GOD PRINTS

Bible FU

DOWN IN FRONT CHILDREN'S SERMONS

ON BIBLE PEOPLE, PLACES AND THINGS

WRITTEN BY
Susan Martins Miller

© 2004 by Cook Communications Ministries

All rights reserved. No part of this book may be reproduced without written permission, except for brief quotations in books and critical reviews. For information, write Cook Communications Ministries, 4050 Lee Vance View, Colorado Springs, CO 80918.

First printing 2004

1 2 3 4 5 6 7 8 9 10 09 08 07 06 05 04
Printed in the United States of America

Edited by: Lois Keffer

Illustrations by Aline Heiser
Cover Design by Peter Schmidt and Scot McDonald, Granite Design
Interior Design by Dana Sherrer, iDesignEtc.

Unless otherwise noted, Scripture quotations are taken from the Holy Bible: New International Readers' Version®. Copyright 1998 by International Bible Society. Used by permission of Zondervan Publishing House. All rights reserved.

ISBN: 0781440831

Table of Contents

IT'S A JOB

Introduction

Blow the shofar. Measure an omer. Share a cloak. Sing a song of remembrance. Tie God's Word around your fingers. Huh?

The Bible can be baffling to kids, until you bring it alive with fascinating bits of history and culture that make the characters seem like real people. These children's sermons take your kids on exciting adventures through Bible times where they'll discover that Bible places were real towns full of real people. Your kids are not too young to understand what daily life was like in the Bible, and they're plenty curious. Ordinary everyday events jump off the pages as kids learn faith lessons from the things that people in the Bible did every day.

Down in Front! Children's Sermons leads you on an exploration of Bible times that winds through four categories:

- **Places & Spaces:** What did Bible time people use caves for? Why was the River Jordan so important? What was the wilderness really like? Travel with your kids through the geography and topography of the Holy Land.

- **Stuff & Things:** How much is an omer and why does it matter? How many coats did Bible time people have? Are baskets good for something more than being pretty? Find out about the tools of daily life and how Bible time people used them.

- **Days of Our Lives:** Where did people stay when they traveled? Did they really walk around on the roof? What's the big deal about Passover? Put yourselves in the shoes of ordinary Bible time people and join in their celebrations.

- **It's a Job:** What did the priest do for the people? Why did Israel want a king? Why did people need scribes? Look at the occupations of Bible time people to enrich kids' understanding of Bible passages.

Each children's sermon has a Bible Truth, Bible Verse and Godprint. Add in some details about life in Bible times, and you have the makings to give your kids an enriching understanding of the Bible stories they're learning in your children's ministry. They'll look at Bible stories with a brand-new perspective when you bring Bible times to life with these sermons.

You can present these sermons with a few simple supplies. Just follow the easy format:

On Your Mark!

Check out the Bible Truth and Godprint to focus on what you'll teach. You're building godly character—helping kids be more like God!

Get Set!

Gather your supplies and bookmark the key verse.

Go!

Gather your kids and take off for Bible time adventures. The bold print tells you exactly what to say to the kids. You can put these concepts in your own words if that is more comfortable for you. You'll see opportunities to involve the whole congregation scattered throughout the sermons, and maybe you'll come up with a few ideas of your own. Remember, everyone is listening, and the children's sermon may be a high point of enjoyment and learning for adults too!

Make your children's sermons count—for everyone. Don't be afraid to get down on the floor with the kids. Listen sincerely to answers when you ask a question. Get a little silly—and grab attention so you can point kids toward God.

You're learning right along with your kids. As you prepare, open your own heart to the message God has for you. After all, we never stop growing more like Jesus.

Susan Martins Miller

Places and Spaces

Phoenicia

Galilee

Decapolis

Judea

Nabateans

Safety Rock

On Your Mark

Bible Truth: We can ask God to help us in times of trouble.

Bible Verse: Show me your favor, God. Show me your favor. I go to you for safety. I will find safety in the shadow of your wings. There I will stay until the danger is gone. Psalm 57:1

Godprint: Prayerfulness

Get Set

You'll need a Bible and a large blanket or bed sheet. Optional: rain stick. Mark Psalm 57:1 in your Bible and keep the blanket just behind you as you begin.

GO!

As children gather, act as though you're scanning the skies. **Looks like a storm is brewing. Yes, sir, we're going to get a big one this time.** Put your hand to your ear. **Do you hear that? The pitter patter is starting.**

Start patting your lap or knees gently and have the kids join you in making the sound of a gentle rain.

I have a feeling it's going to get a lot worse. Pat your legs harder and faster. The kids will follow your lead. **We'd better run for shelter. We don't want to get caught out in this storm. Let's head for that cave over there.** Reach behind you and grab the blanket. Unfurl it so it covers as many kids as possible. Encourage everyone to scrunch in together. Wait for the rain sounds to stop naturally.

I think we're safe in here. This is so much better than being out there in that dangerous storm. While you're in the "cave," talk about:

- What do you do when you're in a dangerous situation?
- What makes you feel safe?

Remove the blanket. **Israel has a lot of caves. In Bible times, people used caves for shelter and safety. Some of the caves were even good enough to live in! They kept people warm and dry and safe. David hid in a cave when King Saul was chasing him and trying to kill him. The prophet Elijah went into a cave when he was running away from angry King**

Ahab. While Elijah was hiding, God spoke to him in a gentle whisper. David and Elijah were both great heroes who did wonderful things. When bad guys were after them, they both hid in caves and waited for the danger to pass.

Did you know that the Bible tells us where we can go for safety? Right here in the Book of Psalms. Ask a volunteer to read Psalm 57:1.

- Where does this verse say we can go for safety? *(To God; to the shadow of his wings.)*
- What do you think "shadow of your wings" means? Does God really have wings?

David probably wrote these words when he was hiding in a cave from King Saul. The king was jealous and angry with David and wanted to hurt him. While he was safe in the cave, away from the danger, David was thinking about who really keeps him safe—God. When we're in danger, God's power covers us like wings that we can hide under—like a safe cave where danger won't find us. God spreads his wings over us to keep us safe. David is saying that he wants to stay under God's protection until the danger is gone.

- When will you ask God to keep you safe?

The next time you snuggle under a blanket the way we did in our dangerous "rain storm," I hope you'll remember to ask God to spread his wings over you and keep you safe. Let's pray now.

Bow for prayer. **Dear God, thank you for being our safety rock. Help us to remember to go to you for safety and stay close to you until the danger is gone. In Jesus' name, amen.**

Of Walls and Towers

On Your Mark

Bible Truth: God wants us to come to him in times of danger.

Bible Verse: The name of the LORD is like a strong tower. Godly people run to it and are safe. Proverbs 18:10

Godprint: Trust

Get Set

You'll need a sledgehammer or baseball bat. Mark Proverbs 18:10 in your Bible.

GO!

Hold up the sledgehammer or baseball bat.

- How many of you think you could knock a hole in the wall of a building all by yourself?
- How many think you could do it if you had the help of all the other kids and a lot of baseball bats?
- How about if you had the help of everyone in the congregation?

If we tried to knock a hole in the wall, we'd find out just how strong the wall is. Well, we're *not* going to knock a hole in the wall today. But we are going to think about strong walls.

In Bible times, buildings weren't the only things with walls. Cities had walls, too.

- Why do you think a Bibletime city would need a wall? *(To keep the people safe. To keep the enemy out.)*
- How big do you think the wall around a city would be? *(Let kids speculate.)*

Let's see if we can imagine how thick the walls of a city would be in Bible times. We need about 20 people to line up behind each other. Ask for volunteers to start a line. If you have less than 20 children, pull some teenagers or adults from the congregation until you have a line of 20 people, one behind the other.

Stand back and admire the thickness of your "people wall." **Wow, that's one thick wall! City walls** were made out of brick or stone. It would take a lot of people with a lot of hammers and baseball bats to break through a wall that thick.

Put your hand on the head of the smallest person in the line. **How high do you suppose the walls were? This high?** Move your hand to someone taller. **This high?** Move to the tallest person in the group. **This high? City walls were about as tall as four grown-up men standing on each other's shoulders—and as thick as this wall of people. Sometimes part of the city wall was a tower that was even higher and stronger than the rest of the wall. If an enemy army was attacking, everyone made sure to run to the wall or to the tower so they would be safe inside.** Have everyone in the wall sit down again.

Let's read a Bible verse about running to a tower. Ask a volunteer to read Proverbs 18:10.

- What does this verse say is a strong tower? *(The Lord; the name of the Lord.)*
- Who runs to this tower? *(Godly people; people who believe in God.)*

God doesn't want us to trust a wall to keep us safe, no matter how thick the wall is. He wants us to trust him. He wants us to run to him when we're in danger.

- How would you run to God? *(Pray; remember Bible promises.)*

Let's pray and ask God to help us trust him. Bow for prayer. **Dear God, you are our strong tower. You are the one we can trust, no matter what is happening. Help us remember to run to you to keep us safe when we're in danger. Amen.**

By the Sea

On Your Mark

Bible Truth: God tells us how we can please him.

Bible Verse: Once again Jesus went out beside the Sea of Galilee. A large crowd came to him. He began to teach them. Mark 2:13

Godprint: Faithfulness

Get Set

You'll need a picnic blanket, spray bottle and a fishing rod or stick and string. Put a bookmark at Mark 2:13 in your Bible. Optional: sticks and strings for everyone.

GO!

Spread out the picnic blanket and encourage as many kids as can fit to join you there. **What a lovely day for a visit to the seaside. Can't you just feel the mist as it comes off the lake?** Gently spray water over some of the kids. **I think this is a great day for fishing, don't you?** Get out your fishing pole and dangle it out in front of you. **Ah, there's nothing like the restful sound of water slurping and slapping along the shore. Slurp, slurp, slap, slap.** Encourage the kids the join you in making water sounds. **Slurp, slurp, slap, slap.** Spray some more water.

- What's your favorite memory of going to a lake?
- What do you like to do at the lake?

Stand up and look out at the congregation. **Wow, there's quite a crowd gathered here today. Why do you suppose all these people are here?** Gently spray people in the first couple of rows. **Let's make some crowd noises. Say, murmur, murmur, murmur.** Pause and let kids make some noises.

Oh, I think the crowd is bigger than that. We'll need everyone to help. All together now: murmur, murmur, murmur.

Assign the kids and the congregation to two large groups. Have one group say "slurp, slurp, slap, slap" while the other group says, "murmur, murmur, murmur." If you'd like, continue gently spraying water. Give a hand signal when you'd like everyone to stop.

Jesus spent a lot of time at a lake called the Sea of Galilee. Talk about great fishing! There were about 30 little towns around the Sea of Galilee, and a lot of people in those towns made their living by fishing. There may have been about 100,000 people living in those towns. You might want to compare 100,000 to the population of your town or city.

You could always count on a crowd around the Sea of Galilee. Jesus did! By the Sea of Galilee was one of his favorite places to teach and meet people. Ask a volunteer to read Mark 2:13.

- What does this verse say Jesus did? (Went out by the sea; taught the people.)
- Mark says, "once again" Jesus went out to the sea. Why do you think he says that? (To show that Jesus had a habit of going to the Sea of Galilee. He went more than one time.)
- If you were in the crowd, what would you want Jesus to teach you about?

Jesus taught the people so they would know that God cares about them, and so they would know how God wants them to live. Mark is one of the writers who wrote down what Jesus said so that we can know how God wants us to live, too. In Jesus' time, people learned about God by going to the lake and listening to Jesus. Jesus was glad to welcome them. He's glad to welcome us too.

- Where do you go to learn about God?

Taking time to learn what Jesus said is a choice that pleases God. Every day we can make choices that please God and show that we're being faithful to God.

- What choices can you make each day that show you're being faithful to God?

Let's pray and ask God to help us know how to be faithful to him.

Bow for prayer. Dear heavenly father, help us to pay attention to what Jesus teaches. Show us the choices you want us to make to please you today. In Jesus' name we pray, amen.

On Jordan's Banks

On Your Mark

Bible Truth: We can believe that God will keep us strong.

Bible Verse: He will be like a tree that is planted near water. It sends out its roots beside a stream. It is not afraid when heat comes. Its leaves are always green. Jeremiah 17:8

Godprint: Conviction

Get Set

Mark Jeremiah 17:8 in your Bible. Optional: poster board or newsprint, marker.

GO!

How many rivers can you name? Let kids rattle off the names of as many rivers as they can. They may name rivers in your area or others in the nation. If you'd like, jot down the names on poster board as kids call them out. Invite adults in the congregation to add to the list. Someone may call out the Jordan River in Israel.

Where would we be without rivers? Up a creek, perhaps! No, I guess there wouldn't even be any creeks if we didn't have rivers.

- Why are rivers important? *(They give us water; they are a way to travel; they water the plants.)*
- What do you think it would be like to live in a place that didn't have enough water?

Let's make a river scene. Mmm. First we'll need a river. Have half your kids form a "river." If you have just a few kids, have several lie down on the floor in a pattern that twists and turns. If you have a lot of kids, have some sit in pairs, bus-style, in as many rows as you'd like.

Now we have our river. What should we put along the banks of the river? Choose some more children to arrange as bushes and trees along the banks of the river. Have "trees" stand with their "branches" up, and have "bushes" scrunch down to the floor. Other children can be animals. Encourage them to make motions and sounds. You can even pull others out of the congregation to add to your scene. Make it as simple or elaborate as you like.

Now tell me: What is the most popular river in the Bible? If the kids don't come up with it, someone in the congregation is sure to say, "Jordan." **You're not just any river. You're the Jordan**

River, which is mentioned 200 times in the Bible. **Imagine for a moment that the Jordan was all dried up. If you're a tree or a bush, let me see you wilt. If you're an animal, let me see you look hungry and thirsty.** Pause for a moment.

Imagine there's wilderness all around. Everywhere you look is dry. The land is dry. The mountain is dry. No water. No rain. Pause for a moment.

Now imagine the mountains are covered with snow, and when spring comes and the snow melts, the water flows down through the river bed. Let me see you come back to life. After a moment, thank everyone and have them sit down again.

Ask a volunteer to read Jeremiah 17:8.

- What happens to a tree planted near water?
- What happens when it gets hot and there's no rain?

God's Word says that the person who depends on God is like a tree planted near water.

- How does God "water" us?

If God is our river of life, we can be sure we'll never dry up and wilt. No matter what happens to us, if we depend on God, he'll keep us strong. The Bible is God's book for us. He wants us to "drink" from it every day. It refreshes us by telling us God loves us. It makes us grow strong by reminding us of what we believe and how to live.

- When is a good time for you to "drink" from God's Word?

Bow for prayer. **Dear God, you give us everything we need. Without you, we would dry up. Thank you for giving us your Word to help us grow strong in our love for you. Thank you for being with us and keeping us going even when we feel like wilting. Thank you for watering us with your strength. In Jesus' name, amen.**

Old and Gray

On Your Mark

Bible Truth: God wants us to tell others about what he does for us.

Bible Verse: God, don't leave me even when I'm old and have gray hair. Let me live to tell my children about your power. Let me tell all of them about your mighty acts. Psalm 71:18

Godprint: Commitment

Get Set

You'll need props to dress up as an elderly person. Mark Psalm 71:18 in your Bible. Ahead of time, ask a teen or adult to dress up and briefly tell the story of how God led his people safely across the Red Sea as it appears below.

GO!

- What's something you remember from when you were really little?
- Have your parents told you any stories about when they were really little? How about your grandparents?

Give two or three kids a chance to share brief stories. **I've invited a special guest to tell us an amazing story today—a story that God's people have been telling for thousands of years.** Have your actor enter and tell this story:

A long, long time ago, God's people were slaves in Egypt. But God had other plans for his people. He wanted to give them a new land. But first they had to get away from the Egyptian army, and that meant they had to get across the Red Sea. This was no easy feat, let me tell you. The Red Sea is nearly 1,200 miles long. You can't just walk around it. You have to get across it, and with an army chasing you, that's a real challenge. But this was no problem for God. He just blew a mighty wind that pushed back the water, and the people walked through the sea on dry ground. Did I mention this was a long, long time ago? God's people have been telling this story for generations, so that no one will ever forget how great God's power is. You can read all about it in Exodus, chapter 14. It's a great story, don't you think? I hope that when you're old and gray, you'll tell the story to some kids you know.

Thank your guest. **God did a great thing for his people when he parted the waters of the Red Sea so they could cross on dry ground. God's people have been telling this story for thousands of years. Remembering things that happened to us when we were younger can be great fun. But remembering the things that God has done for us is even better. Let's read a Bible verse about remembering.** Ask a volunteer to Read Psalm 71:18.

- What does this verse say we should remember to tell?
- Why is it important to remember and tell?

Let's name some of the mighty acts of God that we can tell others about. After each one, we'll say together, "God, you're great." Invite the children to name some mighty acts of God, in the Bible and in their own lives. After each one, respond together, "God, you're great."

Bow for prayer. **Great God, nothing is too hard for your power. Help us to see your power in our lives and remember to tell others about you. In Jesus' name, amen.**

Big as the Sea

On Your Mark

Bible Truth: Nothing is more powerful than God.

Bible Verse: But LORD, you are more powerful than the roar of the ocean. You are stronger than the waves of the sea. LORD, you are powerful in heaven. Psalm 93:4

Godprint: Awe and wonder

Get Set

You'll need a globe or world map. Mark Psalm 93:4 in your Bible. Optional: conch shell that sounds like the sea.

GO!

Who can find the Mediterranean Sea on this globe? Pause while someone finds the sea. Have a child keep a finger on the Mediterranean. **Now I need someone to find Israel.** Have another child put a finger on nearby Israel. **Now what about Egypt, the place where God's people were slaves?** Add another finger on Egypt. **And let's not forget Rome, the place where Paul was a prisoner.** Add a fourth finger on Rome.

It's getting crowded on this globe, isn't it? That's because so many events in the Bible happened in places near the Mediterranean Sea. This was the biggest body of water that people in the Old Testament knew about. They called it "The Sea." Thank your volunteers and have them sit down.

- How many of you have been to the ocean?
- Was it hard to swim? Why? *(The waves.)*
- Was it hard to hear? Why? *(Too much noise.)*

When we stand on the beach next to the ocean, we realize how vast and powerful the sea is! It's hard to imagine anything on earth that's more powerful.

The Bible talks about how powerful the sea is. When God's people went into the promised land, the Mediterranean Sea was the border on the west side. When Jonah was thrown

into the sea and swallowed by a great fish, it was the Mediterranean. When Paul took a long journey to Rome, he crossed the Mediterranean. This was THE SEA in the Bible. If you have a conch, pass it around now and let kids hear the "roar" of the sea.

When I count to three, I want you to make the loudest, sea-roaring sound you can. Ready? One, two, three! Roar with your kids. If you'd like, encourage the whole congregation to roar like the sea.

When the sea-roaring dies down, ask a volunteer to read Psalm 93:4.

- What does this verse say about God's power?
- If the sea is the most powerful thing on earth, and God is more powerful, what does that tell us? (Nothing is more powerful than God.)

God's power isn't just in the stories in the Bible. We see God's power when we look at the ocean today, or when we look at the sky filled with stars at night, or when we see a beautiful brand-new baby. And we see God's power in our lives when he helps us solve our problems and gives us just what we need. Can you think of some ways that God shows his power to you? Pause and let children respond. Let's thank God for his power.

Bow for prayer. Almighty God, nothing is more powerful than you, not even the roaring waves of the sea. We're amazed at how powerful you are, and we're amazed that you use your power to help us. Help us to worship you. Amen.

In the Middle of Nowhere

On Your Mark

Bible Truth: God can give joy in any situation.

Bible Verse: The desert and the dry ground will be glad. The dry places will be full of joy. Flowers will grow there. Isaiah 35:1

Godprint: Joy

Get Set

You'll need some dead or wilted flowers and a dish towel. Mark Isaiah 35:1 in your Bible.

GO!

As you begin, hide the flowers under the dish towel.

- Name an occasion when someone gets flowers. *(Mother's Day, birthday, Valentine's Day, etc.)*
- Have you ever given someone flowers?

Flowers are a great way to celebrate special occasions, or just to say that we appreciate the person we give the flowers to. They seem to cheer up everyone who looks at them. Since we're having such a terrific day, I thought I'd bring in some flowers to celebrate. Remove the dish towel and pick up the flowers. **Aren't they gorgeous**? Sniff the wilted flowers. **Mmm. Such a delicious fragrance. Who would like to smell?** Let the curious ones smell for themselves. **In fact, why don't I share my flowers with some of you?** Start passing out flowers. If you have enough, give every child a wilted flower.

No doubt some of the children will comment about the condition of the flowers. Put on your best pouting face. **I think some of you don't care much for my beautiful flowers. What's wrong with them?** Pause for kids to respond.

- Why do these flowers look like this?
- What could have kept them from looking this way? *(Leaving them in the ground. Putting them in water.)*
- Where do the best flowers grow? *(In a garden; in a meadow.)*
- What about a desert? Could these flowers grow there? *(Probably not.)*

Some plants grow in the desert, but most flowers need a lot more water than they would get in the desert. The Bible talks a lot about the desert, or the wilderness.

- Can you think of a Bible story that happened in the wilderness? *(The Israelites wandered in the wilderness for 40 years before entering the promised land.)*
- What do you think the wilderness was like?

God's people spent 40 years living in the wilderness before they went into the new land God promised them. They were in the wilderness because they had sinned against God. God took care of his people while they lived in the desert, but they still looked forward to the day they could go into the new land. And for generations, even after they went into the promised land, they remembered the time they spent in the wilderness. They learned that even in the desert, God can bring joy. Let's read a verse about that.

Read Isaiah 35:1 and the first part of verse 2: "The desert and the dry ground will be glad. The dry places will be full of joy. Flowers will grow there. Like the first crocus in the spring, the desert will bloom with flowers."

- What do these verses say will happen in the desert? *(They'll be glad, full of joy; flowers will grow.)*
- What's so amazing about the desert blooming with flowers?

Maybe sometimes you've felt like you were in a desert—all dried up, like nothing was going right and nobody cared. You didn't think you had anything to be joyful about. God can bring joy in any situation. He can make flowers grow in the desert, and he can give you joy, no matter what's happening. Let's ask God for that joy.

Bow for prayer. **Dear God, thank you for giving us joy in any situation. When we feel all dried up and like we're living in the wilderness, help us remember that you can make the desert bloom with flowers. Make joy bloom in our hearts. Amen.**

Of Trees and Tongues

On Your Mark

Bible Truth: God wants us to treat others with respect.

Bible Verse: A tongue that brings healing is like a tree of life. But a tongue that tells lies produces a broken spirit. Proverbs 15:4

Godprint: Respectfulness

Get Set

Mark Proverbs 15:4 in your Bible. Optional: Gather pictures of a variety of trees.

GO!

I'm going to say some words. You tell me what they all have in common. Ready? Chestnut, olive, fig, tamarisk, cypress, wormwood, willow. If no one guesses that these are all trees, keep going with some more common varieties: cedar, oak, pine, fir, palm.

Trees! You probably never go a day without seeing a tree of some sort—maybe even hundreds of them at a time if you visit a forest. If you have pictures of trees, let kids look at a few of them b.

- What good things do we get from trees? (Wood to build with and make paper; fruit; syrup; shade; homes for animals; oils.)
- What not-so-good things might come from trees? (Broken branches that could fall and hurt us; creepy crawly things.)

The Bible mentions trees almost 300 times and names around 30 different kinds of trees. But one of the most famous is the "tree of life." When God created the world, he put the tree of life right smack in the middle of the Garden of Eden. We read about that in Genesis, the first book of the Bible. When we get to last book of the Bible, Revelation, we read about the tree of life again in a description about heaven.

- What do you think "tree of life" means?

The tree of life stands for the way we can live forever with God. Can you think of anything

that could be like a tree of life? Pause for responses, then ask a volunteer to read Proverbs 15:4.

- What does this verse say is like a tree of life?
- What does "a tongue that brings healing" mean?
- What's the opposite of a tongue that brings healing? *(Lying.)*
- What is a "broken spirit"?

Show me your tongues! Stick out your own tongue. Let everyone giggle for a moment. **Okay, back in your mouths now.**

- Do you think you could tie your shoes with your tongue?
- How about button your shirt?
- What about make your bed?

There are a lot of things your tongue just can't do! But there are a lot of things it can do, like lick a stamp on a get well card, or taste the cookies you're making for a friend, or say something nice to someone who needs cheering up. Your tongue can also say something mean or tell a lie. Tongues are so little and pretty and pink. They look so harmless, but they can really hurt people.

Proverbs 15:4 reminds us that God wants us to use our tongues for good purposes. We can treat other people with respect by what we say to them. When I point to you, say something nice about someone next to you. Point to as many children as you have time for.

Bow for prayer. **Father, you created the trees of the forest and you created our tongues. Help us to use our tongues to be trees of life so other people can know you better. In Jesus' name, amen.**

Come to the Water

On Your Mark

Bible Truth: If we know Jesus, we have everything we need.

Bible Verse: It was the last and most important day of the Feast. Jesus stood up and spoke in a loud voice. He said, "Let anyone who is thirsty come to me and drink." John 7:37

Godprint: Thankfulness

Get Set

You'll need a pitcher or jug of water, some paper cups and a tray. Mark John 7:37 in your Bible.

GO!

How many of you have used water for something today? Pause and let kids respond. They may mention having a drink, taking a bath, washing clothes, giving water to a pet, watering grass or plants, or cooking. **Now suppose you didn't have any water. The pipes coming into your house are all dried up. In fact, all the pipes all over town are all dried up. No one has any water in their houses. How will we do all these things we need water for?** Pause and let kids speculate. Someone may suggest digging a well.

A well! That's what we need—and of course a good bucket to get the water out of the well. We take water for granted. We just expect it to be there when we turn on the faucet. In Bible times, people didn't have faucets to turn on, but they still needed water. So they went to the well.

- Whose job do you think it was to get the water the family needed?
- What do you suppose was the busiest time at the well?

Every village or city had a well. Usually it was built up with stones all around it for extra safety. The women had the job of going to the well to get the water that their families needed. They would go early in the morning and then again just before sunset and carry jugs of water back to their homes. Sometimes they might see some shepherds at the well getting water for their sheep. On a hot, dry, dusty day, everyone was glad for the water that came from the well.

Begin pouring cups of water and setting them on a tray. **Is anyone thirsty? Jesus had something to say about water. It was Feast time in Jerusalem, and there were a lot of extra people in the city. The wells must have been very busy.** Ask a volunteer to Read John 7:37. Keep pouring water as you talk about:

- What kind of "thirsty" was Jesus talking about?
- How is Jesus like a well that never runs out of water?

Just like the people in Bible times, we need water every day, not just for washing clothes or taking baths. We need to drink water and get it inside our bodies. That's where it does the most good to keep us healthy and feeling good. And that's where we want Jesus to be, too—inside us, keeping us spiritually healthy and feeling good.

Is anybody ready for a drink? If you are, come and drink. Begin passing out cups of water. **As you take this drink of water, remember that Jesus is the living water. When we know Jesus, we have everything we need to keep our hearts from getting thirsty. Let's thank him for that.**

Bow for prayer. **Dear Jesus, thank you for being a well that never runs out of water. Thank you for quenching the thirst we have on the inside. Thank you for filling us up with living water so that we can know you better. In your name we pray, amen.**

Meeting on the Mountain

On Your Mark

Bible Truth: God is worthy of honor for his greatness.

Bible Verse: Honor the LORD our God. Worship at his holy mountain. The LORD our God is holy. Psalm 99:9

Godprint: Praise

Get Set

You'll need a length of rope long enough to tie around as many children as possible. Mark Psalm 99:9 in your Bible. Optional: hats, water bottles and other mountain climbing gear.

GO!

As children come forward for the children's sermon, begin tying loops of rope around their waists so they're all connected to each other. If you have a lot of kids and not enough rope, just have them hang onto the rope with one hand. Look up as if you're viewing a tall mountain from close up. **Have you seen that mountain? We've got a serious climb ahead of us today. We need to make sure everyone is tied together securely before we head up.** Keep looping the rope around more kids. If you have hats, water bottles or other gear, distribute them among the kids.

Let's see, what mountain do you think this is? It might be Mt. Ararat, where Noah's ark came to rest. It might be Mt. Sinai, where Moses received the Ten Commandments from God. It might be Mt. Carmel, where Elijah proved that God is more powerful than Baal. It might be the mountain where Jesus ascended into heaven. It might Mt. Moriah, where Solomon built the temple to worship God.

Let's get climbing. Lead the kids around in a winding path covering as much space as you have. Come back to the spot you started from.

Here we are at the top. What a spectacular view! Put your hand to your eyes and scan the horizon; encourage the kids to do the same. **I feel like I can see forever from up here. Makes me want to worship God. How about you?** Have the kids sit down.

A few minutes ago I named a bunch of mountains from the Bible. What do all those

mountains have in common? Pause to see if any kids want to respond. **In Bible times, the mountain was a place where God's people went to meet with him. That's what they all have in common. Important things happened on the mountain that helped the people know God better and understand how he wanted them to live. When Solomon built a temple for the people to worship God, he built it on a mountain. Let's read a Bible verse about worshiping God on a mountain.**

Ask a volunteer to read Psalm 99:9.

- What does this verse say about why we should worship God?
- What does it mean to honor God?

Have you ever stood on top of a mountain or a big hill and hollered? Maybe you wondered if your voice would echo across a canyon. Maybe you were just so happy you couldn't keep quiet a minute longer! Maybe you wanted to praise God for the beauty that you saw all around you. Let's stand on top of our holy mountain right here and praise God. I'll say a sentence, and you echo it back across the canyon. Lead the children in praise statements. Here are a few suggestions:

> Praise God for his greatness.
> Worship the Lord, all the earth.
> The Lord is king of the world.
> Shout to the Lord with joy.
> Let everything on earth praise the Lord.

If you have time, lead the children "down" the mountain and come back to the same spot. If you prefer, close with prayer at the "top" of the mountain.

Bow for prayer. **God, you are great. You deserve all the honor we have to give. We worship you in our hearts. Help us to show the world that we love you. In your name, amen.**

Something Small, Something Great

On Your Mark

Bible Truth: God can make something great from something small.

Bible Verse: The LORD says, "Bethlehem, you might not be an important town in the nation of Judah. But out of you will come a ruler over Israel for me. His family line goes back to the early years of your nation. It goes all the way back to days of long ago." Micah 5:2

Godprint: Hope

Get Set

You'll need a map that shows some very small towns. Mark Micah 5:2 in your Bible.

GO!

If you live in a very small town, you might have fun during this sermon talking about your own hometown.

Name some famous people who are alive now. Pause to let kids respond. Let them talk about any kinds of famous people who come to their minds: politicians, musicians, actors, athletes and so on. Choose one of the famous people they mention.

Now tell me what you know about this person when he or she was your age. Pause for responses. Very likely, the children will not know anything about the famous person's childhood.

- When someone is six or eight or ten years old, can we know that the person will be famous someday?
- Do you think any of you will be famous someday?

Sometimes famous people come from not very famous places. A little boy named Jimmy was from a little town called Plains, Georgia. Only about 600 people lived in that town. Not very many people had ever heard of Plains, Georgia. But then Jimmy became famous, and Plains, Georgia became famous. Jimmy grew up to be president of the United States, President Jimmy Carter. After he was president, he went on to win the Nobel Peace Prize. His work helped a lot of people.

Take out your map and ask a few kids to find some small towns. If necessary, show them how to look for the small dot or small writing that indicates that a town is very small. If your own town is small, locate it on the map. **There might be a boy or girl in one of these small towns who is going to grow up to do something great. Maybe you are going to grow up to do something great for God. Let's read a Bible verse about that.**

Ask a volunteer to read Micah 5:2.

> • Was Bethlehem an important town?
> • What does this verse say happened in the small town of Bethlehem? *(A ruler over Israel came from Bethlehem.)*

Bethlehem was a small town. It wasn't famous like Jerusalem. It was just a place where people stopped to rest on their way to Jerusalem. But some important people came from Bethlehem. The first ruler to come out of Bethlehem was David. What do you remember about David? *(He was a shepherd; he fought Goliath when everyone else was afraid; he became king of Israel.)*

David was a shepherd boy from the little town of Bethlehem. He became the second king of Israel and one of the greatest leaders the people ever had. Hundreds of years later, after many generations, where was Jesus born? Pause. **That's right, in Bethlehem. And why were Mary and Joseph in Bethlehem?** *(Because of the census; everyone had to go to the hometown of their family, and Joseph's family was from Bethlehem; Luke 2:1–4.)*

Jesus was born in the same family line as David. The verse we read talks about Jesus, too: "His family line goes back to the early years of your nation." Jesus' family line went all the way back to David in Bethlehem.

Christmas is a time of surprises. You shake a box and rattle a package and you're just not sure what's inside. As you open your gifts this year and think about the surprises you find inside, remember one of the greatest surprises of all. A little town like Bethlehem, not important at all, gave us the Savior of the world. God can make something great from something small.

Bow for prayer. **Dear God, thank you for sending Jesus to be the Savior of the world. Thank you for making something great from something small. Give us hope that you will do something great in our lives. Amen.**

Hosanna!

On Your Mark

Bible Truth: Jesus deserves our true worship.

Bible Verse: So they took branches from palm trees and went out to meet him. They shouted, "Hosanna!" "Blessed is the one who comes in the name of the Lord!" "Blessed is the King of Israel!" John 12:13

Godprint: Worship

Get Set

Make copies of the palm branch on page 32 and cut out the leaves. Mark John 12:13 in your Bible. Optional: use real palm branches or make enough copies of page 32 to pass out to the whole congregation.

GO!

As kids come forward for the children's sermon, hand them copies of the palm branch on page 32 or real palm branches. Ask someone to read the words on the branch: "Jesus deserves our true worship."

You're going to help with the children's sermon today. Whenever you hear me say, "Jesus deserves our true worship," you respond with "Hosanna in the highest!" and wave your palm branch. Let's try that. Practice a time or two until you're sure kids will respond confidently.

We're ready to put our story into action. Your real job is to help everyone here today do what you just did and worship Jesus. Please go stand in the aisles between the people and get ready to lead them. If you have real palm branches or extra copies of the reproducible, have kids pass them out to members of the congregation as they stand in the aisles. Help kids get evenly spaced in the aisles.

In Bible times, Jerusalem was an important city. It was the capital of Israel, so a lot of important events happened there. It was also the place where all the people came to worship at the temple. Three times a year, everyone traveled to Jerusalem for one of the great feasts. Jesus was on his way to Jerusalem for the Passover feast when he did something unusual. He told his disciples to bring him a colt, a young donkey. If anyone asked why they were taking the donkey, they were supposed to say, "The Lord needs it." Jesus deserves our true worship. (Hosanna in the highest!)

Let's find out what happened when the crowd saw Jesus coming. Read John 12:13.

- What did the people say when they saw Jesus coming?
- Why were they saying that?

Jesus rode the donkey into Jerusalem. When the people saw him, they praised him as if he were the king. They knew that when a king rode a donkey, it meant he was coming in peace. Many people had heard about the miracles Jesus had done. They thought he was going to save them from being ruled by people they didn't like. *Jesus deserves our true worship.* (Hosanna in the highest!)

Jesus really was the king! But he was a different kind of king than the people thought. He was a king who could save them from their sin, not just from their enemies. Jesus saves us from our sins, and he's the king of our hearts. *Jesus deserves our true worship.* (Hosanna in the highest!)

Great job! Hold your palm branch over your head while we thank God for being a great king.

Bow for prayer. **God, you are our great king. You deserve the best worship that we can give you. We praise you from the bottom of our hearts. Hosanna in the highest! In Jesus' name, amen.**

My Coat, Your Coat

On Your Mark

Bible Truth: God wants us to share what we have with others.

Bible Verse: Suppose someone takes you to court to get your shirt. Let him have your coat also. Matthew 5:40

Godprint: Generosity

Get Set

You'll need six or eight coats of various types—or more if your group is large. Mark Matthew 5:40 in your Bible.

GO!

As kids gather, spread out the coats around you. Put one of the coats on. **Do you like my coat? This is one of my very favorite coats.**

- What are coats for? *(Kids will probably answer that coats are for keeping warm or dry.)*

I'm going to name some kinds of coats. If you have the kind of coat I name, raise your hand. List as many different kinds of coats and jackets as you can think of, pausing for kids to raise their hands. Here are some suggestions:

- wool coat
- winter jacket
- play jacket
- a coat to wear when you're all dressed up
- windbreaker
- raincoat or slicker
- sports jacket
- sweatshirt jacket with a zipper
- denim jacket
- lightweight or summer jacket

I have quite a few coats here. I certainly can't wear this many coats at one time. So I have plenty to share. I'll share these coats with some of you. What I want you to do is

think of something to do with the coat other than wear it. Choose some children to give the coats to. Encourage them to be creative in what they do with the coats. They can do anything from sitting on a coat to using it as a superhero cape. Then collect the coats again. If you have time, let more children take turns with the coats.

You raised your hands a few minutes ago to show that you have different kinds of coats that you use for different kinds of occasions. Then we tried to think of all the different things we could do with a coat. In Bible times, most people only had one coat, or cloak, and they used it for all sorts of things. Someone who was cold would put on a coat. A mother might wrap her baby in her coat. A man might carry his tools in a bundle in his coat. At a picnic, people might sit on their coats. A shepherd in the field at night might use his coat for a pillow or a blanket. Someone who needed a loan might give his coat as proof that he would pay back the money. Wealthy people might have more than one coat or coats from fancy fabrics, but for most people, a coat was the most important piece of clothing they had. Let's read a verse about coats.

Ask a volunteer to read Matthew 5:40.

- What does this verse say we should do with a coat?
- What do you think this means?

You might not think you have any shirts or coats worth fighting about in court. But if you lived in Bible times and you had only one coat, you might think differently. This verse is about being generous when no one expects it. Instead of getting back at someone, give something extra! That's God's way.

He wants us to be generous even with the things that are important to us and even when it might not seem fair.

How often do you put on a coat? The next time you do, maybe you'll remember this verse and think about being generous.

Bow for prayer. **Dear Lord, you give us everything we need. Help us to remember that so we can be generous and give something extra in your name. Amen.**

Optional: Use this children's sermon as an opportunity to launch a coat drive. Ask the congregation to bring in coats in good condition to share with people in your community who need them. Partner with a local organization that can help you find the people who need the coats you collect.

A Basket Full

On Your Mark

Bible Truth: God wants us to think about what other people need.

Bible Verse: Suppose you are gathering your crops. Then do not harvest all the way to the edges of your field. And do not pick up the grain you missed. Leave some for poor people and outsiders. I am the LORD your God. Leviticus 23:22

Godprint: Unselfishness

Get Set

You'll need a small basket, small wrapped candies, CD player and CD. Mark Leviticus 23:22 in your Bible.

GO!

Pass out wrapped candy to the children as they assemble, one piece per child. If you have extra candy, drop it in the basket.

Sweets for the sweet! Have a piece of candy—just don't unwrap it yet!

- What would you like to do with the piece of candy I just gave you? *(Eat it! Save it for after lunch.)*
- How would you feel if I said I wanted you to give your candy away?

Mmm. I wonder if we have enough candy to fill up this basket. Why don't we find out? When I start the music, we'll pass the basket around. When it comes to you, put your candy in the basket. Keep passing the basket until the music stops. Here's the trick—you don't have to pass it to the person next to you—pass it across the circle or in any direction you'd like. Play music until all the children have put their candies in the basket. Stop the CD.

Pick up the basket of candy and look at it studiously. **How did we do? Is it full?** (That depends on the size of your basket!) **We're going to pass the basket again. This time, when the basket comes to you, take a piece of candy (don't open it yet!). Then pass the basket on to someone else who doesn't have a piece yet.**

Play basket-passing music until everyone has a piece of candy.

- Do we have any leftovers? *(Let kids look to see if any candy remains in the basket.)*
- What do you think we should do with these leftovers? *(Pass the basket again. Give some to other people.)*
- What do you use baskets for in your home?

These days we have all sorts of containers for holding things: plastic tubs, cardboard boxes, tin cans. So we often use baskets just for decoration. But in Bible times, people needed baskets for all sorts of things. Can you think of some Bible stories with baskets? *(Baby Moses; the feeding of the 5,000; Paul's escape.)*

Jesus fed 5,000 people with a little boy's lunch—and there were plenty of leftovers to put in baskets! Sometimes there were leftovers in a field at harvest time. Workers harvested the field by tying the grain up in bundles, but they didn't always get every single piece of grain. Sometimes there were leftovers. God told the people what he wanted them to do with the leftovers. Have a volunteer read Leviticus 23:22.

- What does this verse say the harvesters should do?
- Who will pick up the leftovers?

The owners of the land could have said that all the grain belonged to them, even the pieces that fell on the ground. But God wanted them to think about what other people might need—people who didn't own land or have enough food for their families. Let the baskets at your house remind you that God gives us what we need with some left over to share with others.

Bow for prayer. **Dear God, thank you for leftovers and baskets. When we have leftovers and baskets, help us to remember that we can be unselfish and think about what someone else might need. In Jesus' name, amen.**

Horns of Worship

On Your Mark

Bible Truth: We can show God that we love him and honor him.

Bible Verse: Shout to the LORD with joy, everyone on earth. Burst into joyful songs and make music. Make music to the LORD with the harp. Sing and make music with the harp. Blow the trumpets. Give a blast on the ram's horn. Shout to the LORD with joy. He is the King. Psalm 98:4–6

Godprint: Praise

Get Set

Mark Psalm 98:4–6 in your Bible. Optional: kazoos, noisemakers or rhythm instruments for all the kids.

GO!

Is church a place to make noise? If you vote no, hold up your hand. If you vote yes, hold up your foot! Pause to let kids respond.

You might be thinking, what a strange question! And what a strange way to vote yes! We come to church to worship God. Do we make noise when we worship God? Pause and let kids answer. **Some noise is bad, and some noise is good. For instance, when we come to church and sing together to praise God, that's good noise! What other kinds of noises do we make when we praise God?** (Praying aloud. Talking. Making music.) **Let's look at some verses in the Bible that talk about making noise when we worship.**

Ask a volunteer to read Psalm 98:4.

• What does this verse say we should do? (Shout to the Lord; burst into songs; make music.)

When I count to three, everyone give a shout to the Lord. You can say something like, "God, you're great!" or "Praise God!" Ready? One, two three!

Ask a volunteer to read Psalm 98:5.

• How does this verse say we should worship God? (More music! Sing; play the harp.)

If you have kazoos, noisemakers or rhythm instruments, pass them out now and take a minute for the kids to make their own kind of music!

One more verse. Have someone read Psalm 98:6.

> • How does this verse say we should worship? *(Blow trumpets; shout.)*

This verse talks about a special instrument, the ram's horn. Another name for this is the shofar. This was a kind of a trumpet made from an animal's horn. It wasn't the kind of trumpet that plays melodies or fanfares. It only had a few notes. It was the kind of trumpet that gave a special signal, like the beginning of one of the big feasts that God's people celebrated, or a call to battle, or to let people know about important announcements—or to call people to worship. Let's imagine we're playing the ram's horn. Show kids how to put their hands together in front of their mouths as if blowing a ram's horn and make a long, low sound.

That's our signal. Time to praise God! When we praise God, we show him that we love him and honor him, whether we shout or sing or play the harp or blow the trumpet. Let's thank God for all the ways we can make noise when we praise him.

Bow for prayer. **Dear God, you are the king of the whole earth. We want to show that we love you and honor you. Thank you that we can shout and sing and make music to praise you. Amen.**

On the Move

On Your Mark

Bible Truth: We can obey God because he is always with us.

Bible Verse: Here is what I am commanding you to do. Be strong and brave. Do not be terrified. Do not lose hope. I am the LORD your God. I will be with you everywhere you go. Joshua 1:9

Godprint: Obedience

Get Set

You'll need a simple tent you can set up or a large blanket and a few folding chairs. Mark Joshua 1:9 in your Bible.

GO!

If you have a camping tent you can set up quickly without stakes, kids will enjoy helping you set it up. Or you could set it up partially ahead of time and just have kids help put the last few poles in place. If you don't have a tent, a blanket and folding chairs will work just fine. Either way, you'll be picking up the tent and moving it.

As the kids assemble, look around. **Let's see, where should we set up camp? This looks like a good spot right over here. Maybe a few of you could help me with this.** Get the tent set up and have everyone sit on the floor in front of it. (You might want to be sure to zip the door if you don't want kids exploring the inside of the tent while you talk, or position yourself in front of the door.)

As everyone gets settled, begin looking around as if you're dissatisfied. **Mmm. Maybe it would be better over there.** Point to another location, even if it's only a few feet away. **What do you think? Yes, I do believe we should move the tent over there.** Get everyone up on their feet and have some of the kids take poles (or chairs) and move the tent to a new location.

Get everyone settled again, then move the tent once more. This time kids may be a little suspicious about getting comfortable, but encourage them to sit down in front of the tent.

In the Old Testament, when God's people were living in the desert and didn't have a country of their own, they worshiped in a tent called the tabernacle. God told Moses just how to put the tent together. It was made in a way that was easy to take apart, pack

up and move to a new location. **The people moved around in the desert for 40 years, but everywhere they went, the tabernacle was the first thing they set up. Then the people would camp around all four sides of the tabernacle. The tabernacle was a sign that God was with his people wherever they went.**

Ask a volunteer to read Joshua 1:9.

- What does this verse promise? *(That God will always be with his people.)*
- What does this verse tell us not to do? *(Be afraid; lose hope.)*

God's people were on the move! They didn't have houses; they lived in tents. They didn't have a building to worship God in; they had the tabernacle. But none of that mattered. No matter where God's people went, God was there first. He went ahead of them to lead the way so they didn't have to be afraid.

- How can this verse help you?

We don't have the tabernacle any more, but we do have God's presence. He's always with us, leading the way, so we don't have to be afraid. Let's pray.

Dear God, thank you for being with us, whether we live in a tent or a house or a mansion. Thank you that everywhere we go, you are already there. In Jesus' name, amen.

Pop a couple of the key poles in your tent and have a couple of kids help you carry it out.

Where Does Light Come From?

On Your Mark

Bible Truth: God's presence and care make us glad from the inside out.

Bible Verse: LORD, you keep the lamp of my life burning brightly. You are my God. You bring light into my darkness. Psalm 18:28

Godprint: Joy

Get Set

You'll need a bowl of cold spaghetti noodles and a dish towel. Mark Psalm 18:28 in a Bible. Optional: blindfold

GO!

Make sure that the towel is covering the bowl of noodles before kids come close to the front.

Wave both your arms in the air if you *love* not being able to see where you're going. Nod your head up and down if you *love* trying to find your way down a path when it's pitch dark. Stand up if you *love* waking up in the middle of the night and feeling scared because you can't see. Pause here if any children seem to want to talk about how they feel in the dark. If any children stood up, make sure everyone is seated again.

We can't make this room completely dark in the daytime, but if you close your eyes, you can imagine you're in the dark. Let's try that. Pause to make sure that all the kids close their eyes. **That's right, squeeze 'em tight.**

* If you get nervous in the dark, what's the first thing you do? (*Open your eyes. Turn on a light. Call for Mom or Dad.*)

Open your eyes. I need a volunteer to reach for something in the dark. Choose a child. (If your group is large, you may want to invite a couple of children to do this simultaneously.) When the child's eyes are closed, pull out your bowl of cold spaghetti and place it within reach. Guide the volunteer's hand to find the spaghetti. Eyes are sure to pop open! Your volunteer can sit down now. Offer the dish towel for a quick clean up.

You never know what you'll stumble into in the dark—even a yucky bowl of cold noodles! It's a good thing to have light. **Where do we get the light for this room?** Let kids point out light fixtures and windows.

- If you're out camping, where do you get light from? *(Flashlights, campfires, lanterns.)*
- If you're looking for your lost soccer ball in a dark closet, where do you get light from?

We get a lot of our light from electricity and batteries. In Bible times people didn't have those things. They used oil lamps for light. A lamp was probably made out of clay, with a place to pour oil into it, and a place to put a wick. When the wick was lit, it would make the oil burn and give off light. It was important to keep the lamp burning all the time. If it went out, someone would have to get a flame from somewhere else to start it again. Sometimes women got up during the night to make sure the lamp had enough oil and wick to keep burning till morning. At the temple, a special lamp burned in the holy place to remind the people that God was always with them.

The Bible has a lot of verses about lamps. Let's read one. Ask a volunteer to read Psalm 18:28.

- According to this verse, where does light come from? *(God.)*
- What do you think "lamp of my life" means? *(God gives us life; God keeps us going in tough times; inside happiness.)*

God is with us and takes care of us. That makes us glad from the inside out, even when it's dark all around us. He doesn't just give us light for a room, but light for our whole lives. We don't have to worry about getting up in the dark to refill our lamps, because God does it for us. Let's thank God for that.

Bow for prayer. **Dear God, thank you for keeping the lamp of our life burning. Thank you for bringing light into our darkness. Help us to remember that our light comes from you. Amen.**

Stings and Scents

On Your Mark

Bible Truth: No matter what happens, we know God is in control.

Bible Verse: "Death, where is the battle you thought you were winning? Death, where is your sting?" 1 Corinthians 15:55

Godprint: Hope

Get Set

You'll need several small fragrant pouches, such as potpourri, or cotton balls with various scents added. Put a spot of vanilla, cinnamon oil, fresh orange, fresh lemon, aloe or other perfume on each cotton ball. Also keep on hand some dry cotton balls and a scent you can add later. Mark 1 Corinthians 15:55 in your Bible.

GO!

As kids assemble, begin passing around the fragrant pouches or scented cotton balls. If you used familiar scents, invite kids to guess what the scents are. If you have time, suggest that kids take the cotton balls to the congregation to get some guesses. After all guesses are in, tell them the right answers and collect the pouches or cotton balls.

- Tell me something we could use these delicious fragrances for. *(Make the room smell nice; use like perfume.)*

In Bible times, people had a special use for spices and perfumes. They used them when someone died. In the part of the world where we live, we usually bury someone who has died. At the time when Jesus lived on earth, someone who died was put in a cave instead of in the ground. But before that happened, friends would use a lot of spices and perfumes on the body. The Bible tells us that Jesus' friends did this for him. You might want to ask someone to read John 19:39–40. **His friends Nicodemus and Joseph wrapped his body in cloth with a lot of spices. Then they put Jesus in a tomb that was carved out of a rocky hillside, and covered the tomb with a huge stone.**

That was on Friday night. What happened on Sunday morning? Pause and let kids recount the story of Easter morning. Then recap.

On the first Easter morning, some other friends of Jesus wanted to take more spices to the tomb. But the tomb was empty! Jesus wasn't there, because he wasn't dead any longer. His friends knew for sure he had died. A whole crowd of people saw it happen. They had no hope that he was alive. But he was! God was in control, even when Jesus died, and he had an amazing surprise for all of Jesus' friends—he raised Jesus from the dead.

Ask a volunteer to read 1 Corinthians 15:55.

> • What does this verse tell us about death? *(It doesn't really win. God wins.)*

The Easter story reminds us that no matter what happens, God is in control. Our hope comes from God himself, not from anything good or bad that happens to us. When Jesus rose from the dead, God made a way for us to be with him forever. Even though our bodies might die, we can live with God in heaven—all because of what Jesus did.

Let's pray and thank God for giving us hope. Bow for prayer. Dear God, you are more powerful even than death. You raised Jesus from the dead. Thank you for being in control, no matter what happens to us. Thank you for giving us hope. Amen.

Take out the dry cotton balls and bottle of vanilla or other scent. I'm going to give you each a cotton ball that smells really good. What can this cotton ball help you remember? *(The Easter story; Jesus died and rose again.)*

As I hand you a scented cotton ball, I want you to say, "God is in control." Then take your cotton ball back to your family and tell them, "God is in control." You might want to ask an adult or teenager to help you scent and pass out cotton balls.

Written in Stone

On Your Mark

Bible Truth: God's Word tells us how he wants us to live.

Bible Verse: The Lord finished speaking to Moses on Mount Sinai. Then he gave him the two tablets of the covenant. They were made out of stone. The words on them were written by the finger of God. Exodus 31:18

Godprint: Obedience

Get Set

You'll need play dough, a rolling pin and a cutting board. Mark Exodus 31:18 in your Bible. Optional: extra play dough in zip-top bags.

GO!

As kids assemble, roll the play dough around in your hands to soften and shape it. If you have a large group, use plenty of play dough.

I'm thinking of writing a letter, or maybe a story, or maybe a whole book. I think I have all the supplies I need, don't you? Pause. Some kids are sure to object that you can't write a letter on play dough; you need paper and a pencil.

Once you have the play dough softened, ask for a volunteer or two to help you roll it out flat and smooth on the cutting board. Be careful not to get it too thin.

Let's see. Who should I write my letter to? Choose a child's name, and say, "Dear _____" as you begin to write in the dough with your finger. **The great thing about writing a letter in play dough is that you can let it dry and keep it for a long, long time**. Let kids lean in and see how you have written in the dough with your finger. If you have time and enough play dough, you might let kids try it for themselves.

If you wanted to write a letter, you might get out a piece of paper or a nice card. In Bible times, long ago, people really did write on clay and stone. Did you know that even God wrote on stone?

Ask a volunteer to read Exodus 31:18.

- What does this verse say God gave Moses? *(Two tablets of the covenant, the Ten Commandments.)*
- What did God use to write on the tablet? *(His finger.)*

Wow! God had a message for his people, and he wrote it down with his own finger. The tablets that God gave Moses that day were the Ten Commandments. God gave the Ten Commandments so his people would know how he wanted them to live.

- What do you think it would be like to see something that God wrote with his own finger?
- We don't have those stone tablets today. How do we know how God wants us to live? *(Read the Bible, God's Word.)*
- What's the best part of obeying God and doing the things he wants us to do?

The next time you use play dough or any other kind of clay, maybe you'll remember how we tried to write a letter in the clay. Then you'll remember that God wrote on stone with his own finger because he wanted his people to know how to obey him. Let's ask God to help us obey his Word.

Bow for prayer. **Dear Father, we don't have those stone tablets, but we do have your Word. Thank you for telling us how you want us to live. Help us understand your Word and obey you. In your name we pray, amen.**

That's Not Junk

On Your Mark

Bible Truth: God is faithful to us; we can be faithful to him.

Bible Verse: Never stop reading this Scroll of the Law. Day and night you must think about what it says. Make sure you do everything that is written in it. Then things will go well with you. And you will have great success. Joshua 1:8

Godprint: Faithfulness

Get Set

You'll need a small paper scroll and the contents of a junk drawer. If you don't have a junk drawer, just gather an assortment of small items: coupons, paper clips, index cards, rubber bands, string, small toys. Anything will do. Put the "junk" in a paper bag. Write "Joshua 1:8" on the scroll, roll it up and add it to the junk bag. Mark Joshua 1:8 in your Bible.

GO!

As kids gather, begin rummaging through your junk bag as if you're looking for something intently. Pull out one item at a time and say things such as, "I haven't seen this in years. I wondered what happened to it." "I don't even know what this is." "Why do you suppose anyone would keep this broken old toy?" Invite a few kids to reach in with their eyes closed and pull out some items. Continue making exasperated comments about how useless everything in the bag is. If a child pulls out the scroll, suddenly act very interested. Or reach in and pull out the scroll yourself.

What's this? This doesn't look like a broken old toy. Maybe this is something we can use. Ask a volunteer to unroll the scroll and read what's written inside. Joshua 1:8. **That sounds like a Bible verse. We'd better look it up.**

Ask as volunteer to read Joshua 1:8.

- What does this verse tell us to do? *(Keep on reading the Scroll of the Law. Do everything it says.)*
- What is the "Scroll of the Law"? *(God's Word.)*

In Old Testament times, people didn't have Bibles to hold in their hands like we do. But

they did have God's Word. In those days "books" were written on scrolls. The Scroll of the Law was God's Word. The words on the scroll told the people how God wanted them to live.

But sometimes the people didn't pay attention to God's Word written on the scroll. Sometimes they even lost the scroll. The Bible tells us about a time when King Josiah wanted to clean up the temple so the people could worship God. While the workers were cleaning, they found something that was lost in a pile of junk, just the way we found a scroll in our pile of junk. They found the Scroll of the Law that our Bible verse talked about.

King Josiah helped the people remember Joshua 1:8. He helped them remember to keep on reading God's Word and keep on doing what it says.

- Why do you think it's a good idea to keep on reading God's Word?
- How does reading God's Word show that you really want to follow him?

God cares for us and tells us how he wants us to live. We can show that we care for God by choosing to live his way. Let's thank God for showing us his way.

Bow for prayer. **Dear God, you gave us your Word so that we would know how to follow you. Help us to keep on reading your Word so that we can please you and follow your way. In Jesus' name, amen.**

Silence Please

On Your Mark

Bible Truth: God is great! We can show respect for his power.

Bible Verse: "But I am in my holy temple. Let the whole earth be silent in front of me." Habakkuk 2:20

Godprint: Reverence

Get Set

Mark Habakkuk 2:20 in your Bible.

GO!

As children assemble, put your finger to your lips and say "Shhh." When everyone is settled, speak in a whisper or a quiet tone.

Have you ever played the quiet game? In the quiet game, the person who stays quiet the longest is the winner. That means no talking and no wiggling. Let's play for just a moment and see how we do.

Pause for as long as a minute if kids are quiet that long. Look around and, without speaking, encourage them to continue being quiet. Even if the kids are quiet, you will probably hear some congregational noises during this time. Take note of what you hear.

Okay, the quiet game is over. Let everyone breathe a sigh of relief. **I heard some wiggly noises from the congregation. It's not always easy to be quiet, even in church.**

- How hard was it for you to keep completely quiet?
- How do you feel on the inside when you keep quiet on the outside?

Sometimes when we come to church we make lots of noise together! We sing joyfully to God, praising and worshiping him. But sometimes at church we want to be quiet and still before God.

In the Bible, God's people worshiped at the temple. King Solomon built the very first temple, and he made it a splendid place, with only the best of everything. He wanted

everyone around to know how great God is. Hundreds of years later, people built another temple and tried to make it even better and greater than Solomon's temple.

- Why do you think Solomon wanted to build a great temple for God?

The temple was a holy place where the people came to worship God. The temple was a place to show respect for how great God is. Let's read a verse about that.

Ask a volunteer to read Habakkuk 2:20.

- Why should the whole earth be silent before God?
- How does being silent before God show respect for God's greatness?

When we're quiet before God, we can think about how wonderful he is. We can ask him to fill us with his love. It's worth it to be quiet before God, even if it's just for a minute. When you think about how great God is and how much he loves you, it changes the way you think about your whole day!

Let's bow quietly before God one more time. This time, say a silent prayer telling God how great he is. Then I'll pray aloud.

Bow for prayer. Allow for a comfortable period of silence for private prayer. **Dear God, you are great and you are holy. There is no one else like you in the whole world. We worship you for your greatness. Thank you for filling us with your peace. Amen.**

Pass the Grace

Bible Truth: We can please God by the way we speak to others.

Bible Verse: Let the words you speak always be full of grace. Season them with salt. Then you will know how to answer everyone. Colossians 4:6

Godprint: Friendliness

Get Set

Prepare a batch of popcorn. Leave the popcorn completely unsalted, with no butter. You'll also need a carton of ordinary table salt. Bookmark Colossians 4:6 in a Bible. Optional: coffee filters or small paper cups.

GO!

Mmm. I'm in the mood for a snack, aren't you? Let's see, do I want something fruity? No, that's not it. How about something sweet? No, I don't think so. Something salty, yes, that would be just the right thing.

Get out the bowl of unsalted popcorn and pop a few in your mouth. **Mmm. Something's not right about this. I can't quite figure out what it is. Maybe some of you should eat some and see if you can tell me what's wrong.** Depending on the size of your group, you may want to offer everyone a taste of the unsalted popcorn. It won't be long before someone will identify that the popcorn is missing the usual salt.

Salt! That's what we need. Let's see, do I have any around here? Pull out the carton of salt and sprinkle some on the popcorn. Offer the popcorn for more tasting. If you prefer, you could have a second bowl of popcorn already salted so that you're sure to have enough to go around. Depending on your setting, you can let kids munch while you talk or set the popcorn aside for now.

- Why does salt make popcorn taste better? (*Salt brings out the flavor of foods.*)
- What other foods do you like to put salt on?

When we go to the supermarket, we can buy a lot of foods with salt already in them. This might be for flavor, or it might be as a preservative to keep the food fresh longer. In

Bible times, people used salt for the same things—to keep food fresh and to make it taste better. There's a place called the Dead Sea that has very salty water, and the hills all around the lake are full of salt. If you could see those hills, you might think you'd never run out of salt. No matter how much salt you like on your snacks, you'd have enough.

In the New Testament, the Apostle Paul has something to say about salt. Let's read that verse. Ask a volunteer to read Colossians 4:6.

- How can words be like salt?
- What do you think the words "full of grace" mean?

We can please God by the way that we speak to others. Do we use words that encourage others? Words that show kindness? Or words that make hurt feelings even worse? Sometimes we're not very careful about the words we say to our family or our friends. We might even be more rude to our friends than we would be to a stranger.

We eat salt every day in all kinds of foods. The next time you have a salty taste in your mouth, remember that God wants your words to be salted with grace when they come out of your mouth.

Bow for prayer. **Dear God, thank you for our friends. Thank you for telling us how we can please you in the way we talk to our friends. Remind us to use words salted with grace. Amen.**

If you'd like, serve up individual servings of popcorn in paper cups or coffee filters that kids can take with them.

An Omer a Day

Bible Truth: We can be generous because God gives us what we need.

Bible Verse: My God will meet all your needs. He will meet them in keeping with his wonderful riches that come to you because you belong to Christ Jesus. Philippians 4:19

Godprint: Unselfishness

Get Set

You'll need a box of cereal (or more if you have a large group), paper cups or coffee filters, several measuring cups and a 2-quart pitcher. Mark Philippians 4:19 in a Bible.

GO!

When you pour yourself a bowl of cereal for breakfast, how do you decide how much to pour? *(By the size of the bowl; by how hungry you feel.)*

What if there is not much cereal left, and your sister wants some, too? *(Some kids may justify taking all the cereal for themselves; others will suggest sharing it.)*

Suppose I want to share my cereal with you. I have a full box, after all. I don't need it all for myself. But I want to make sure everyone gets enough. I want everyone to have the same amount. How can I do that? *(Measure.)*

Ask some of the older kids or an adult assistant to help you measure 1/2 cup of cereal for each child. Serve the cereal in paper cups or coffee filters. While kids are munching, begin talking about the story of manna in the wilderness. **In the Old Testament times, when God's people were living in the desert for 40 years, they got worried about what they were going to eat. But God had a plan. Who remembers that Bible story?** Let kids tell you what they know of the story. God provided manna every morning and quail every night. The people were to gather just what they needed to eat for one day.

• Who can tell me what God's people had to eat while they were in the wilderness? *(Manna; bread from heaven.)*

- How did the people know if they would get enough to eat every day? *(Whatever they took would be enough for the day.)*
- How much food did God tell the people to gather for one person each day?

I'm going to say some funny sounding words. You say them after me. Omer. Pause. **Ephah.** Pause. **Hin.** Pause. **Homer.** Pause. **We use things like measuring cups and spoons when we measure our food. A recipe might say one half cup, or one pint, or two quarts. That tells us how much of each ingredient to add. If we lived in Bible times, we would hear words like omer and ephah, or hin or homer to tell us how much to measure. Archaeologists have found old pots that help us understand those measurements.**

When God's people were in the desert, God told them to gather an "omer" of manna for each person each day. That was about two quarts. Hold up the two-quart pitcher. **God knew how much each person would need. No matter how hungry a person was, an omer of manna was just right. Some people tried to take too much, but the extra food spoiled and they couldn't eat it. God knew just what they needed. An omer a day was exactly right.**

Ask a volunteer to read Philippians 4:19.

- According to this verse, who gives us what we need?
- How does God know how much to give us?

God is generous with us, isn't he? We belong to him, and he wants to take care of us. He gives us the "omer" that we need every day, just like he did for his people in the wilderness. Then it's our turn to be generous. Because God gives us everything we need, we can be generous with other people. We don't have to keep all the cereal for ourselves, even if there is only a little bit left.

Bow for prayer. **Dear God, thank you for taking care of everything we need. Help us to be generous with other people because we know you are generous with us. Amen.**

Better Than Gold

On Your Mark

Bible Truth: We can use what God gives us to honor him.

Bible Verse: It is much better to get wisdom than gold. It is much better to choose understanding than silver. Proverbs 16:16

Godprint: Wisdom

Get Set

Photocopy page 58 on card stock (yellow would be great!) or glue a photocopy to a file folder before cutting out the coins. If you have a large group, make more than one copy. Mark Proverbs 16:16 in your Bible.

GO!

Can you talk with your eyes closed? Pause and give kids a chance to show that they can indeed do this. **Here's what I want you to say: More than silver, better than gold**. Let's try that. Have everyone close their eyes and repeat the phrase. **Great! Keep your eyes closed.**

Now I'm going to put something in the hands of a few of you. When it comes to you, pass it on to someone else. The whole time we're passing, we'll keep on saying, "More than silver, better than gold." Then when I say, "Enough is enough," stop passing. Ready? Put photocopied coins in the hands of several children. Use as many coins as you need to in order for everyone to have a turn passing quickly. When you think everyone has had a chance to handle one of the coins, say, **Enough is enough. Now you can open your eyes. What do you have in your hands?**

You've been passing around some "coins." Do these look and feel like any kind of money you're used to? (No.)

• What do you think it would be like to try to live without using money?

In early Bible times, people didn't use money. They just traded what they had for something that they needed. Later on, they started using coins. We passed around a paper coin. But what are coins really made of? (Metal.) **The kings of some countries would put a special mark on a piece of metal so everyone would know what the coin was worth.**

The Jews had a special coin for paying the temple tax. When Jesus lived on earth, people used coins from places like Rome and Greece. When you hear Bible stories, you might hear words like shekel and denari. Those are coins.

The coins were made out of gold or silver or copper. Which one do you think was the most valuable? *(Gold.)* What was the next most valuable? *(Silver.)*

Gold and silver are still very valuable. In fact, some people think nothing in the world is more valuable than gold and silver. Let's find out what God's Word has to say about that. Ask a volunteer to read Proverbs 16:16.

- What does this verse say is better than gold or silver?
- How can we use money to honor God?
- How can we use wisdom and understanding to honor God?

All the gold in the world won't mean anything if you don't have God's wisdom. And all the silver in world is worthless if you don't understand God's way to live. God wants us to use what he gives us to honor him, whether we have a little bit of money or a lot of money. Let's pray and ask for God's wisdom.

Dear God, thank you for giving us wisdom and understanding. Help us to remember that these are better than gold and silver. Help us to use whatever we have to honor you. Amen.

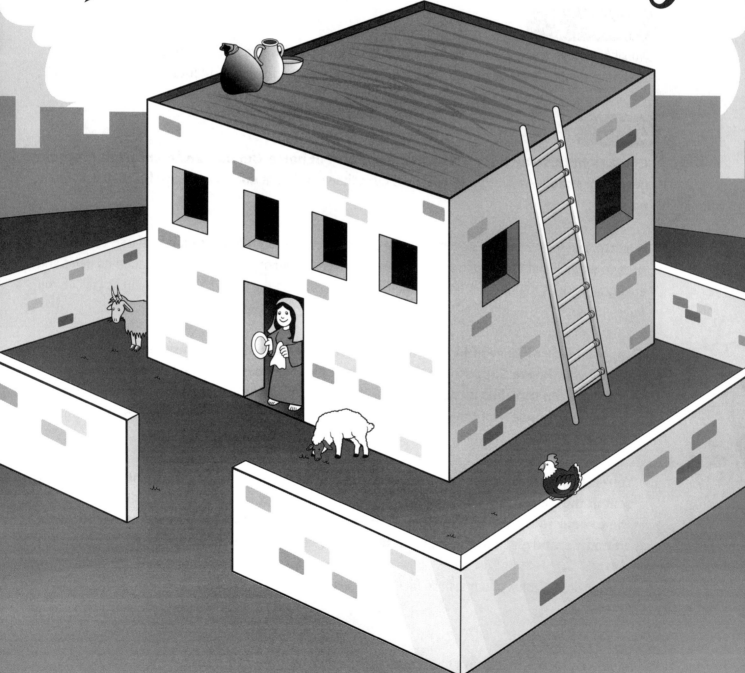

No Complaints Here

On Your Mark

Bible Truth: We can please God by being friendly to visitors.

Bible Verse: Welcome others into your homes without complaining. 1 Peter 4:9

Godprint: Friendliness

Get Set

You'll need a suitcase full of odds and ends of clothing, such as large shirts, sweaters, hats or scarves; and food items that can be passed around, such as crackers or dried fruit. Mark 1 Peter 4:9 in your Bible.

GO!

Come right this way. Have a seat. Make yourself at home. Get nice and comfortable. Let me get you a snack. As kids get settled, pass out a little snack. **We don't want any hungry tummies, no sirree.**

Reach into your suitcase and start pulling out clothing items. **You look like you could use something nice to wear.** Hand a piece of clothing to one of the kids to put on. Keep passing out clothing items and encouraging kids to put them on over their own clothes. Pass the snacks around again as well, if you have enough.

Suppose I didn't live around here and I was on a long trip. Suppose my long trip takes me right by your house. Suppose it's time for supper just as I pass by—and I'm really hungry and tired. I've been traveling all day, and I need some hot food and a place to sleep. So of course I go to your house. Point to one of the children. **Or maybe yours. Or yours.** Point to various children.

You're so glad to have me come to your house while I'm on my trip that you give me your seat at the supper table and make sure that I get the best food. When it's bedtime, you take me to your room and let me sleep in your bed—after you run me a nice, hot bubble bath, of course, and give me the biggest, fluffiest towel you have in the house.

• What do you think of our visit so far? *(Pause and let children respond.)*

- Let's think of some words that describe the kinds of things you're doing for me at your house. (*Friendship, thoughtfulness, generosity, hospitality.*)
- How do you feel when people come to visit your family at your house?

The Bible has something to say to us about people coming to our homes. Let's find out what it is.
Ask a volunteer to read 1 Peter 4:9.

- What does it mean to "welcome" someone into your home?
- When is it hard to welcome someone without complaining?

Welcoming others into your home is a way to show hospitality. In Bible times, travelers often stayed with people in their homes. Sometimes they didn't even know the people they stayed with. If someone came to your house and needed something to eat and a place to stay, you did everything you could to make the person comfortable. You would probably even let the person sleep in your bed or share your clothes.

God's people knew that this is what God wanted them to do. They also knew that God wanted them to show hospitality without complaining. That's the hard part! Having a guest might mean extra work around the house, or waiting until later to do something you want to do, or sleeping on the floor so the guest can have a bed. God wants us to welcome others without complaining. Let's pray and ask God to help us with the hard part.

Bow for prayer. **Dear God, thank you for friendship and for the people who make us feel comfortable. Help us to make other people feel comfortable without complaining. In Jesus' name, amen.**

Collect the snacks and clothing items you distributed earlier.

Planes, Trains and Automobiles—NOT!

On Your Mark

Bible Truth: No matter where we go, God is there to take care of us.

Bible Verse: The LORD himself will go ahead of you. He will be with you. He will never leave you. He'll never desert you. So don't be afraid. Don't lose hope. Deuteronomy 31:8

Godprint: Trust

Get Set

You'll need a map of the country, string, tape, marker and 12 sheets of paper. Mark Deuteronomy 31:8 in your Bible.

Ahead of time, choose two cities on the map on opposite sides of the country, such as Seattle and New York, or Los Angeles and Washington, D.C. Tape one end of the string down at one city and the other end at the other city.

Write each of these numbers on a sheet of paper: 600, 125, 65, 30, 4, 2 1/2. On each of the remaining sheets, write one of these words or phrases: airplane, high speed train, car, horse and buggy, walking, camel. Use large letters so everyone will be able to see.

GO!

Ask a couple of volunteers to hold up the map so everyone can see it. **Wow, according to this map, we have a long trip ahead of us**. Point out the string between cities. **What are some different ways we could get from this city to this city?** Pause and let kids respond with transportation ideas.

Recruit some more volunteers to hold up the papers with words. **Here are some transportation ideas. But how fast are they?** Hand out the sheets with numbers to other children or people in the congregation. **Match up the numbers with the type of transportation. How fast do you think each kind of transportation can go?** When everyone agrees on the matches, tape the words and numbers together. The correct answers are: plane (600), high speed train (125), car (65), horse and buggy (30), walking (4), camel (2 1/2).

It looks like we're ready for our trip now. We have a map showing us where to go, and we

can choose how we want to go. If we decide to walk, we're going to need a lot of sneakers! If we choose a camel, we'll need a lot of patience!

We might think it's funny to think about traveling so far on foot or with a camel. But in Bible times, traveling was no joke! It was slow, uncomfortable and dangerous. People used camels and donkeys to carry their things and often walked beside the animals. God wanted his people to know that no matter what kind of journey they took, no matter where they went, he would be with them. Let's read a verse about that.

Ask a volunteer to read Deuteronomy 31:8.

- What is your favorite part of this verse?
- What does it mean to "lose hope"?

When we lose hope, we think no one cares about us. We feel like we can't trust anyone to take care of us. But this verse gives us a good reason not to lose hope. God is with us! And he'll never leave us. No matter what road we're on, what city we travel to, or what kind of transportation we use, the Lord goes ahead of us and leads the way. We can trust him to care about us, no matter what. Let's thank God for caring about us.

Bow for prayer. **Dear Lord, thank you for going ahead of us and leading the way. Thank you for being with us all the time. Help us not to be afraid, and help us not to lose hope, but to trust you to take care of us. We pray in Jesus' name, amen.**

Our Daily Bread

On Your Mark

Bible Truth: Jesus is the way that we can know God forever.

Bible Verse: Then Jesus said, "I am the bread of life. No one who comes to me will ever go hungry. And no one who believes in me will ever be thirsty." John 6:35

Godprint: Faith

Get Set

Gather several different kinds of breads, such as various rolls, pita bread, bagels, an uncut loaf, sandwich bread. Set the breads on a tray, and cover the tray with a towel. Mark John 6:35 in your Bible. Optional: if your set-up permits, have some bread dough that kids can knead or roll out, or unbaked pizza crust to spread in a pan. Or, put bits of refrigerated biscuit dough in zip-top bags for kids to handle.

GO!

How many times a day do you eat bread? Name the times. Pause and let kids respond. They may mention toast for breakfast, a sandwich at lunch, rolls with dinner. If they don't think of more uncommon forms of bread, ask them about things like pizza crust, hot dog buns, doughnuts, coffee cake, muffins and so on. Then show your tray of breads and pass out bread dough if you have it.

- What's your favorite kind of bread?
- Where do you get your bread?

Most of us buy our bread at the supermarket, or perhaps at the bakery if it's a special kind of bread. Once in a while, we make our own bread. We mix the flour and water and yeast and other ingredients, wait for the bread dough to rise, then bake it in the oven. Mmm. Yummy! There's nothing like warm, homemade bread fresh from the oven.

Begin passing your tray of bread around. Invite children to tear off a piece of whatever kind of bread they prefer. If time permits, encourage children to pass the tray to people in the front rows of the congregation.

Maybe you've learned in school about the food pyramid. What's the biggest food group

that we should eat from each day? *(Bread and grain.)* **When it comes to bread, not much has changed since Bible times. In those days, like now, bread was an important part of daily living. People ate bread every day, several times a day.**

When God's people were in the wilderness, God sent bread from heaven so the people would have something to eat every day. Do you remember what that was called? *(Manna.)*

In the New Testament, Jesus fed a crowd of people with five small loaves of barley bread. Do you remember how many people? *(5,000.)* **Later the people went to find Jesus to ask him about the bread that comes from heaven. Let's find out what Jesus said.**

Ask a volunteer to read John 6:35.

- What do you think Jesus meant when he said, "I am the bread of life"?
- According to this verse, what happens to the person who comes to Jesus?

Retrieve your tray of breads. **Suppose I had a whole tray of bread and you were very hungry. Imagine I said, "Just look at my bread, and you won't feel hungry anymore. You don't actually have to eat any." Would that work? Of course not.**

But how do we feed our spirits? By eating bread—the bread of life. When we have faith in Jesus and ask him to be part of our lives, he satisfies a special hunger inside us, the hunger to know God. Jesus is the way that we can know God forever, starting right now. Let's thank him for that.

Bow for prayer. **Dear Jesus, you came to earth to show us the way to heaven. You are the bread of life. You help us to know God and live with him forever. Thank you for satisfying the special hunger inside us. In your name we pray, amen.**

Worship with the Best

On Your Mark

Bible Truth: When we worship God, we give him our best.

Bible Verse: Praise the LORD for the glory that belongs to him. Bring an offering and come to him. Worship the LORD because of his beauty and holiness. 1 Chronicles 16:29

Godprint: Worship

Get Set

You'll need a two-piece gift box, wrapping paper, scissors, tape and ribbons or crepe paper in a variety of colors. Plan to wrap the top and bottom sections of the box separately. Also, be ready with scrap paper and a pen. Mark 1 Chronicles 16:29 in your Bible.

GO!

As children gather, bring out the gift box and wrapping paper. **I need some help wrapping this box. I want it to be the best looking gift box anyone ever saw, and I just know that if we all work together we can do a great job.**

Have a couple of kids cut wrapping paper to the right size (or cut it ahead of time yourself), then use tape to wrap the bottom and the lid of the box. Let everyone help by adding a piece of ribbon or crepe paper to the outside of the box.

Take the lid off the box. **Do you know what I want to put in this gift box? I want to give God my best in this box. Let's think of some ways that we can give God the best we can give. I'll write them down and put them in this box.**

Kids may mention giving offerings, prayers, singing songs, loving God, loving others and so on. Write down any ideas they have and put them in the gift box. Then put the lid on.

When we give God our best, we bring an offering of worship to him. In the Old Testament times, God's people brought the best they could bring. God gave them instructions for building a tabernacle so they would have a place to worship him together. All the people brought their best gifts—gold, silver, bronze; blue, purple and scarlet yarn; fine linen, oil and spices, precious stones. They gave God their best so they could worship God together.

Let's read a verse about this.

Ask a volunteer to read 1 Chronicles 16:29.

- What does this verse tells us about why we should worship God?
- How does bringing an offering show worship?

We may not have gold or silver to bring to God. But we can give God the best of ourselves. We can give God our hearts when we worship him. That's the best gift of all. I'm going to leave this gift box up here in front of the church as a reminder that we want to give God our best when we worship him. Let's pray.

Bow for prayer. **Dear Lord, you are beautiful and holy. You deserve glory and praise. Help us to worship you by giving you the best of what we have in our hearts. In Jesus' name, amen.**

On Top of the World

Bible Truth: God is always with us, and he's always in control.

Bible Verse: How can I get away from your Spirit? Where can I go to escape from you? If I go up to the heavens, you are there. If I lie down in the deepest parts of the earth, you are also there. Suppose I were to rise with the sun in the east and then cross over to the west where it sinks into the ocean. Your hand would always be there to guide me. Your right hand would still be holding me close. Psalm 139:7–10

Godprint: Hope

Get Set

Mark Psalm 139 in your Bible.

GO!

What's your favorite thing to climb? Pause for kids to respond. They may mention trees, ladders, playground equipment and so on. **What about a roof?**

- What are some good reasons you would need to go up on the roof of your house? (*Put up Christmas lights, fix a leak, move an antenna around, put up a satellite dish, put on a new roof.*)
- How would you get up there? (*Most likely a ladder, or possibly climb out a second story window.*)

What would you think about living on the roof? On most of our houses, the roof is too steep. If we tried to put a table or a bed on the roof, it would slide right off, and where would we be then?

In Bible times, roofs were different. A roof was like having a patio on top of your house. It was a flat open space. And you didn't need a ladder to get there. You could just take the stairs on the outside of your house. Sometimes people even had a garden up on the roof. Imagine going upstairs to pick some vegetables for your supper! In very hot weather, people would go up to the roof to sleep because it was cooler up there. Sometimes people might even build a small room on the roof. Can you think of a Bible story where that happened? (*A woman in Shunem built a room on her roof Elisha. She put a bed, table, chair and lamp on the roof for him to use. She wanted him to have a place to rest when he came to town. See 2 Kings 4:8–10*).

The Book of Acts in the New Testament tells us that one day Peter went up to the roof

to pray. Maybe he wanted to get away from all the distractions going on inside the house. Maybe he wanted to be alone with God. While Peter was up on the roof, God gave him a vision of something he wanted Peter to do.

Do you ever feel like you'd like to go somewhere just to get away from everything? Maybe you're tired of your sister teasing you, or you're tired of doing chores or homework, or maybe a friend hurt your feelings, or you had a really bad day on the soccer field. Maybe climbing to the roof sounds like a good idea to you.

All of us have times when we feel like we just want to get away from it all. But one thing we never want to get away from is God. Let's read some verses about that.

Ask a volunteer to read Psalm 139:7–10.

- Why can't we ever get away from God? *(Because God is everywhere.)*
- Why is it a good thing that we can't ever get away from God? *(God is in control of everything, and we can trust him to take care of us.)*

Most of us can't go up to a roof to rest and relax and be with God like Elijah and Peter did. But imagine that your heart has a roof, a quiet place. Instead of trying to get away from God's Spirit, let's try to find a quiet place to be with God.

Bow for prayer. **Dear Father, thank you that there is nowhere we can go to get away from you. Thank you that you are with us, wherever we are. Help us to look for places to be with you. Amen.**

Sing to Remember

On Your Mark

Bible Truth: When we share our joy, other people can praise God, too.

Bible Verse: He gave me a new song to sing. It is a hymn of praise to our God. Many people will see what he has done and will worship him. They will put their trust in the LORD. Psalm 40:3

Godprint: Joy

Get Set

Mark Psalm 40:3 in your Bible. Optional: rhythm instruments, noise makers, kazoos.

GO!

I'm glad you're all here, because we have some major celebrating to do today. If you're using rhythm instruments, noise makers or kazoos, pass them out now.

What's your favorite musical instrument? Pretend to be that instrument. When I say "Go," everybody be an instrument. One, two, three, go! If you'd like, encourage the entire congregation to participate. Pause for a moment of chaos! Then give a hand signal to stop.

What about singing? Your voice is a musical instrument. What's your favorite song to sing? Pause for responses. Kids may mention worship songs or popular jingles.

Suppose I said it was my birthday today. What song would you sing? (Happy Birthday.)

Suppose it was Christmastime. What song would you sing? (Kids will name a variety of Christmas songs.)

Suppose we were rooting for our favorite football team. What song would you sing? (Be prepared for some cheers and moans from adults!)

Suppose you wanted to praise God for doing something really great. What would you sing? Pause for responses.

Wow! We celebrate a lot of things by singing. Do you know that people in the Bible did the same thing?

After God delivered his people from slavery by parting the Red Sea, Moses led the people in a song of praise (Exodus 15). **When the angel Gabriel told Mary that she would be the mother of God's Son, she sang a song** (Luke 2). **When Paul and Silas were in prison, even there they found something to celebrate and sang to praise God** (Acts 16). **The last book of the Bible, Revelation, describes God's people in heaven singing a song to praise Jesus** (Revelation 5).

The Bible has lots of verses about songs and singing songs. Let's read one of them. Ask a volunteer to read Psalm 40:3.

- Where did the song in this verse come from? *(God.)*
- What does this verse say happens when people hear a song of praise to God? *(They worship God and trust the Lord.)*
- What happens in your heart when you sing a song to praise God?

Let's name some great things that God has done that we can praise him for. Pause for responses. Invite the congregation to respond as well. Then choose a praise hymn or chorus that your congregation knows well to sing together. Close in prayer.

God, you are great. God, you are wonderful. God, you deserve all our praise. We want everyone to know how great you are. Help us sing songs of praise to help others know how great you are. Amen.

Come One, Come All

Bible Truth: We can share God's love when someone has a special need.
Bible Verse: He felt deep concern for them. He healed their sick people. Matthew 14:14
Godprint: Compassion

Get Set

You'll need an assortment of fresh foods you would normally keep in a refrigerator. Mark Matthew 14:14 in your Bible. Optional: shopping mall brochures or sale ads; wilted or spoiled food.

GO!

If you'd like, you can include the whole congregation in your opening instructions.

If you've been to the mall lately, wiggle your right foot. Pause. **If you've been to the grocery store lately, put your left hand behind your head.** Pause.

Lots of us like to go shopping, don't we? Especially if we have some money to spend! If you think it would be fun to go shopping every day—or even twice a day—show me your silliest face. Pause for responses. **Whether you like to go shopping or not, sometimes it's a necessity. You're out of milk and the milk is at the store, so you have to go there.**

If you have shopping brochures or ads, spread them around in front of you now, or hold them up where everyone can see them. **Sometimes you can get a good deal if you watch the ads. That makes shopping even more fun.**

Take out your refrigerator items. **When you get home from shopping, some stuff can go straight to your room. But where would you put things like these?** *(The refrigerator.)* **What if you didn't have a refrigerator? Bring out some wilted produce or spoiled food items. Mmm. Yummy. Shall we have a snack?** Watch kids recoil!

We're so used to having refrigerators to keep our food fresh that we might not think about what would happen if we didn't. In Bible times, people didn't have refrigerators in

their homes. **But they still needed to eat! If they didn't want to eat food like this** (hold up the wilted food), **they had to go out every day to get the fresh food that they were going to eat that day. They might even go shopping more than once a day. Villages and cities had marketplaces where people could buy food and other items they needed around their homes.**

The marketplace was more than just a place to shop. Since so many people came to the marketplace every day, it was a place to do anything that you needed a group of people for. Children played games there, teachers might teach a class there, and people who didn't have jobs would go there to look for work.

When Jesus came to a marketplace, people would do one more thing—bring their sick friends and family members. Let's read a verse about what Jesus did when he saw the sick people in the marketplace. Ask a volunteer to read Matthew 14:14.

- How did Jesus feel about the sick people he saw?
- What did Jesus do for the sick people?

Jesus had compassion for the people. He knew they were hurting and suffering, and he did something to help them. The next time you go shopping for the things you need, I hope you'll look around and see people the way Jesus saw them. You can even do a "prayer walk" around the store and say a quick, silent prayer for all the people you pass! Let's pray and ask God to help us see people as Jesus saw them.

Bow for prayer. **Dear God, we know that you love all people. Sometimes we think only about ourselves. Help us to think about others. Help us to see what other people need and do what we can to help them. In Jesus' name, amen.**

Say It Again, Please

On Your Mark

Bible Truth: God wants us to love each other because he loves us.

Bible Verse: Here is my command. Love each other. John 15:17

Godprint: Love

Get Set

Mark John 15:17 in your Bible. Optional: poster board to write words on, marker.

GO!

On the count of three, I want you to call out a word that you know how to say in another language. One, two, three! Some kids may have learned some simple counting words; other kids may be fluent in a second language because of home environment or experience living overseas. If you know adults who are fluent in a second language, you might ask them ahead of time to be ready to say some simple phrases or teach a few words to the children.

How many languages do you think there are in the world? Pause and take some guesses. Invite adults to guess as well.

Right now there are more than 6,800 "living" languages in the world. A living language is one that people still speak. Many languages are "dead," meaning that no one speaks them in everyday life any more. But some languages that no one speaks any more are like branches of a family tree. They're related to languages that we do speak. I'm going to say some words from languages, and I want you to repeat them.

Mandatum. (Pause.) **That's an old Latin word.**
Mande. (Pause.) **That's from a language called Old French.**
Maunde. (Pause.) **That's a word from a language called Middle English.**
Mando. (Pause.) **That's a Spanish word that people still use today.**

What do all these words have in common? (They sound alike; they have the same root.) **The first word that I said for you was from Latin, and it means "commandment." What do you think all the other words in the other languages mean?** (They also mean commandment.) **We have an English word that means commandment, too—"mandate."**

Now here's a phrase that we still use in English today. Maundy Thursday. What do you suppose that means? (Commandment Thursday.) **Maundy Thursday is a day when we remember a special command that Jesus gave. He was with his disciples to celebrate the Passover feast, one of the great Jewish holidays when people came to Jerusalem. Passover remembered the time that God saved his people from slavery in Egypt.** Find out what the kids know about the first Passover event. This was the last of the ten plagues that God put on Egypt. Jewish families killed a lamb and spread the blood on the doorposts. When the angel of death came that night, he passed over the Jewish homes but killed the oldest son in the Egyptian homes. Then God's people left Egypt and God took them to a new land. (See Exodus 11–12.)

God wanted his people always to remember what he had done for them by celebrating the Feast of Passover. The celebration lasted several days. The day that Jesus was with his disciples was a Thursday. The next day, Friday, was the day Jesus died. Let's find out one of the last things Jesus said to his disciples before he died. Ask a volunteer to read John 15:17.

- Why do you think Jesus gave his disciples this command before he died?
- Is this a hard command or an easy command to follow? Why?

Jesus was about to die for our sins so we wouldn't have to take the punishment we deserve. He did that because he loved us. His command to his disciples and to us was to love each other, even when it is not easy. Maundy Thursday is a day to remember that command, but God wants us to follow the command every day. Let's pray and ask God to help us remember it every day.

Bow for prayer. **Father, you sent Jesus to live on earth so we would know how much you love us. Love is something for every day, not just one day. Help us to remember Jesus' command and to follow it every day. Amen.**

Surprise Inside

On Your Mark

Bible Truth: We show our relationship with God in our attitudes and actions.

Bible Verse: Guard the truth of the good news that you were trusted with. Guard it with the help of the Holy Spirit who lives in us. 2 Timothy 1:14

Godprint: Responsibility

Get Set

You'll need 50 of any item to count, such as dried beans, buttons, cotton balls, colorful index cards, crackers, spoons from the church kitchen, etc. Any sort of item will do. If you expect very young children to be present for your presentation, choose carefully for safety. You'll also need a colorful box or tin with enough small treats inside for every child to have one. Mark 2 Timothy 1:14 in your Bible.

GO!

Select a child to hold (but not open!) the box or tin of treats.

We've got some counting to do today. (Name of child) **is holding a curious looking box over here.** Ask the child to shake the box. **Something interesting is in there. But if we want to find out what it is, first we have to count. How high should we count?** (Kids may say three or ten.) **Sometimes we just have to say one, two, three. Sometimes we count to 10. This time we're going to count to 50. I have 50** (beans, cards, spoons) **to help us count. When we get to 50,** (name of child) **will open the box. Are you ready?**

Depending on the number of children and their ages, you might choose to involve them in handling the items as you count together. You might have children take turns saying the next number as you point to each child, or have the whole congregation count aloud together. Make sure your volunteer is ready to open the box or tin as soon as the group says 50. Pass out the treats inside and let kids enjoy them as you continue.

In Bible times, 50 was a special number. Fifty days after God's people celebrated Passover, they celebrated another feast. This one was called Pentecost, which means 50. The people celebrated Pentecost every year. The New Testament has an amazing story of what happened one year on Pentecost. We can find this story in Acts 2. The believers

were together in a room, and suddenly a sound came from heaven. It was like a strong wind and filled the whole house. The people saw something that looked like tongues of fire that settled on them. They were filled with the Holy Spirit and began to speak in languages they didn't know!

We counted to 50 and had a surprise treat. They counted to 50 and had a surprise of the Holy Spirit. Now the Holy Spirit lives in people who believe in Jesus. Let's read a verse about that. Ask a volunteer to read 2 Timothy 1:14.

> • What is the truth of good news we've been trusted with? *(Jesus died for us so we can know God.)*
> • What do you think it means to guard this truth?
> • Who helps us guard this good news? *(The Holy Spirit.)*

One of the ways we guard the truth of Jesus in us is in how we act and what we say. Let's do things and show things that let people know that we have the Holy Spirit living in us. Let's use the gifts that God gives us to help others know about him.

Bow for prayer. **Father God, thank you for the good news about Jesus. Thank you for the Holy Spirit who shows us how to live. Remind us that your Spirit helps us show others that we belong to you. In Jesus' name, amen.**

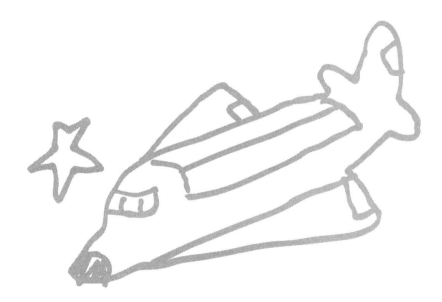

The Right Time

On Your Mark

Bible Truth: We can count on God's strength when we don't have any of our own.

Bible Verse: My help comes from the LORD. He is the Maker of heaven and earth. Psalm 121:2

Godprint: Courage

Get Set

Mark Psalm 121:2 in your Bible. Optional: a clock with hands that you can move.

GO!

Once kids gather, turn to the whole congregation. **Hold up your hand if you're wearing a watch.** Pause. **Hold up your other hand if you have looked at the clock during this church service.** Pause. You'll probably hear some chuckling! Turn to the kids. If you have a clock with moveable hands, let them manipulate the hands while you talk about time.

- What time do you wake up in the morning?
- What time do you eat lunch?
- How do you know when it's time to go to bed?
- How do you know when it's the right time for your spelling test?

Set the clock aside. **Sometimes you might feel like sleeping at school—or even at church—but it's not the right time. Or when recess comes, you're glad it's the right time to go out and shoot some hoops or jump rope. Those are easy choices. But what if you see a bully picking on somebody at recess? How do you know when it's the right time to tell someone who can help?**

The Bible has a story about someone who had to figure out if it was time to tell the king about a bully. We find this story in the Book of Esther. Who can help me tell the story of Esther? Find out what the kids know about this story, then recap it for them.

Esther was a Jewish girl who was chosen by a Persian king to become his wife, the queen. Esther found out about a secret plot by a man named Haman to kill all of God's people, the Jews, on a certain day. She had to decide if it was the right time to ask the king for

help. Even though she was the queen, she still had to wait until the king invited her to see him. If she went without an invitation, she might die. Esther decided it was the right time to go to the king. She asked all the people to pray for three days for God's help. Then she went to the king. He was glad she came, and he helped her. He made a new law that God's people could fight back on the big day. Esther's courage and trust in God saved God's people.

The Jewish people never forgot Esther's courage. They celebrate the big day with a holiday called Purim. During Purim, they remember that Esther found her strength in God and did something that took a lot of courage. Let's read a verse about where we find our strength. Ask a volunteer to Read Psalm 121:2.

- Where does this verse say our help comes from? *(The Lord.)*
- Why do you think this verse reminds us that God is the maker of heaven and earth? *(If God can make heaven and earth, he can do anything.)*

Esther's story shows us that we can count on God's strength when we don't have any of our own. It's always the right time to depend on God for courage. Let's pray.

Lord, you are the maker of heaven and earth. Nothing is too scary for you. When we have to do something that takes courage, help us to remember that we can count on your strength. Amen.

In a Manner of Speaking

On Your Mark

Bible Truth: We can help others know about Jesus by the way we live.

Bible Verse: You make it clear that you are a letter from Christ. You are the result of our work for God. You are a letter written not with ink but with the Spirit of the living God. You are a letter written not on tablets made out of stone but on human hearts. 2 Corinthians 3:3

Godprint: Evangelism

Get Set

You'll need paper, markers and masking tape. Mark 2 Corinthians 3:3 in your Bible.

Ahead of time, write large alphabet letters on sheets of paper. Depending on the size of your group, you may want to repeat some commonly used letters.

GO!

I need to write my friend a letter. But I'm just not sure I can do it all by myself. I'm going to need your help. I need you to be the letters of the alphabet.

Use the masking tape to hang alphabet letters on the backs of kids. If you have a smaller group, tape letters to the front of kids also, or recruit some volunteers from the congregation to be additional alphabet letters.

Okay, I think we're ready to start. I want to say, "Dear Friend." So we need to start with D. Have the child wearing the letter D stand up with the letter facing the congregation. Continue with E, A, R, and F for the beginning of Friend. When you need to repeat letters, such as R, you can either use more kids wearing the same letters, or physically move the child wearing the letter you need to repeat to a new space. Spell out "Dear Friend," and continue with more words as much as space and time allow.

Stand back and look puzzled. **You know, this is turning out to be harder than I thought. I think maybe I'll just send an e-mail. Thanks for all your help.** Ask everyone to sit down.

Turn to the congregation. **How many of you can remember when you didn't have a computer at work or at home? Remember when writing a letter meant getting out a pen and writing on paper and licking a stamp for the envelope?**

In Bible times, writing a letter meant writing on a parchment scroll or even a stone tablet. Imagine how much work that must have been—and how hard it would be to correct a mistake! It was important to make sure you knew what you wanted to say before you started writing. Letters were important. Many of the books of the New Testament were letters that Paul wrote to congregations in various cities.

Let's read a verse from one of Paul's letters. Ask a volunteer to read 2 Corinthians 3:3.

- What was the letter Paul was talking about written on? *(Human hearts.)*
- What was the letter written with? *(The Spirit of the living God.)*

I tried to have you be the letter I was writing. That was hard, because I was just using paper and tape, and you each were just one letter of the alphabet. Imagine what it would be like if you could be the whole letter. That's what Paul is talking about in this verse. Your life can be a letter to other people. When you know Jesus, God's Spirit is inside you, writing a letter from the inside out. Other people can see Jesus shining in you, and they will want to know him, too. Let's ask God to help us be letters for him.

Bow for prayer. **Dear God, thank you for writing on our hearts with your Spirit. Help us to be living letters for you. Help us to show by everything we do and say that we love you, so that others will know how to love you, too. In Jesus' name, amen.**

Take a Break

On Your Mark

Bible Truth: God wants us to take time to remember what he has done for us.

Bible Verse: In six days I made the heavens and the earth. I made the oceans and everything in them. But I rested on the seventh day. So I blessed the Sabbath day and made it holy. Exodus 20:11

Godprint: Thankfulness

Get Set

You'll need a copy of page 84, a pen and some kind of noisemaker you can blow. Mark Exodus 20:11 in your Bible. Optional: blow a real trumpet whether or not you know how to play one!

Before your presentation, arrange for a volunteer to help. Ask your helper to listen for the words, "I could sure use a rest!" and then immediately blow the noisemaker or trumpet.

GO!

Make sure your helper is ready and close by. Your helper may sit in the front row of the congregation or stand to the side of your group.

As kids gather, get set with your calendar page (p. 84) and a pen. **I've had a really busy week. You probably did too. Let's take a few minutes to think about everything we've done this week. Mmm. Let's see. What did we do on Monday?** Encourage kids to list things they did on Monday, such as go to school, soccer practice, piano lesson, shopping, homework, and so on. As they name their activities, write them in the "Monday" space on the calendar page. Write in some of your own activities, or invite people in the congregation to contribute. Then move on to Tuesday. Pace yourself according to how much time you have, but make sure you cover every day from Monday to Saturday.

When you are just about finished filling up Saturday, sigh as if you're exhausted and put down your pen. **I am soooo tired. Just thinking about all the things that we did this week is wearing me out. I could really use a rest!**

Be ready for your helper to blow a horn!

What was that? Pause; kids will point out the source of the sound. **I think that sound is a signal. What could it be a signal for?** Pause for responses.

In the Old Testament, God's people used to listen for signals. One of them was a double blast of a trumpet. This signal came every Friday just as the sun was about to set. It was a signal that the Sabbath was about to begin. People were supposed to stop working! The Sabbath was a day of rest, a holy day. Let's read a verse about it. Ask a volunteer to read Exodus 20:11.

- Who was the busy person in this verse? *(God.)*
- How many days did God work hard? *(Six.)*
- What did God do on the seventh day? *(Rested.)*

This verse tells us that God made the seventh day, the Sabbath, a holy day by resting. A few verses before this, the Bible tells us to remember to keep the Sabbath day holy (Exodus 20:8). **It's pretty easy for us to get really, really busy and try to do lots of things, whether we're playing or working. God wants us to take time to rest and to be with him.**

You might be wondering if we're going to finish our calendar. We filled in spaces for six days, but we didn't fill in the Sunday space. We're going to leave it blank! That will remind us to make the Sabbath a day of rest!

Bow for prayer. **Lord, your Word tells us what you want us to do. Help us to obey. When we get too busy, remind us to slow down and honor you with a day of rest. In your name we pray, amen.**

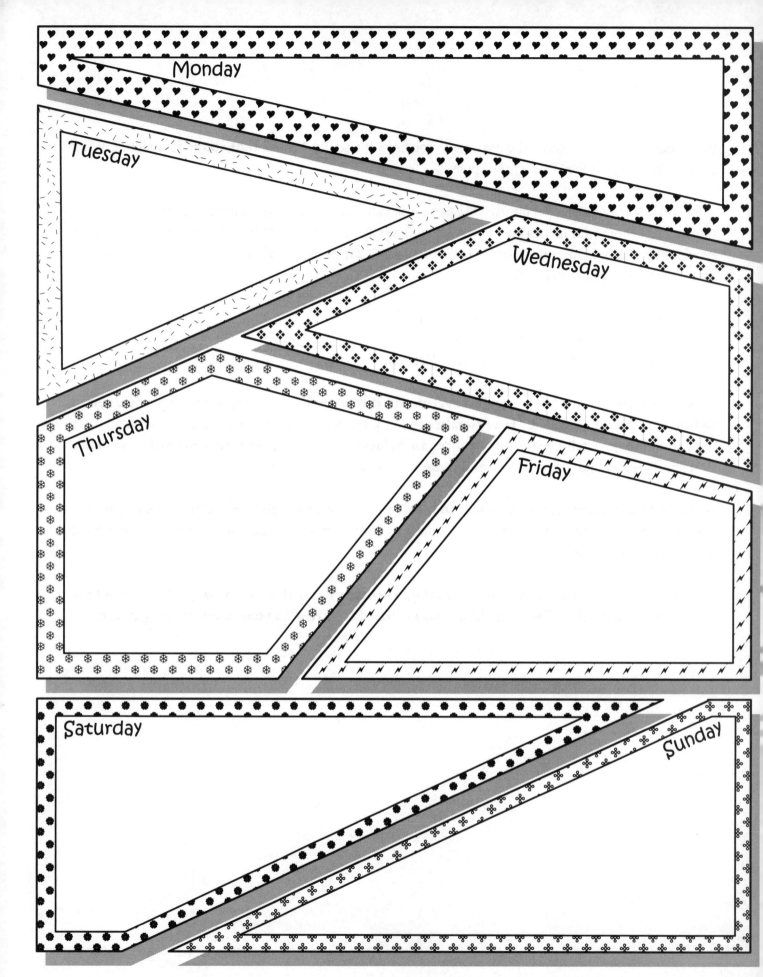

Monday

Tuesday

Wednesday

Thursday

Friday

Saturday

Sunday

The Good Shepherd

On Your Mark

Bible Truth: We can thank God that Jesus loves us enough to die for us.

Bible Verse: I am the good shepherd. The good shepherd gives his life for the sheep. John 10:11

Godprint: Thankfulness

Get Set

You'll need a pet collar, pet food, pet dish and assorted other items related to caring for an animal. If you have a veterinarian in your congregation, ask to borrow some less common items for animal care that may interest the kids. Put all the items in a bag. Mark John 10:11 in your Bible.

GO!

As children gather, begin pulling out the items in your bag one by one. **Let's see, what do we have here?** Let kids identify the items as you reveal them. Then ask:

- What are all these things for?
- What do you think is the most important part of taking care of an animal?
- What kinds of animals have you helped care for?
- Have you ever helped take care of a sheep?

We don't have too many shepherds in our country. But in Bible times, in Israel, being a shepherd was a common job. Can you name some people in the Bible who were shepherds? (Abraham, Jacob, Moses, David, the shepherds who came to Bethlehem. Someone may mention Jesus, the Good Shepherd.)

Shepherding was an important job because sheep gave the people a lot of things they needed: wool, meat, milk. Even the sheep's horn was used as a container for oil or as a trumpet. The shepherd's job was to make sure the sheep had enough food and water and a safe place to rest. Sometimes there was plenty of pasture near the village. But sometimes the shepherd had to take the sheep further away, where they might run into lions, bears, hyenas or jackals.

- If a bigger animal tried to hurt your pet, what would you do? Why?

You would fight for your pet because you love your pet. You might even think that it would be better if a big dog bit you than to let it hurt your little kitten.

Shepherds faced danger all the time. They had to decide how much they cared about the sheep. Did they care enough to get hurt themselves? Did they care enough that they were willing to die to keep the sheep safe? In Bible times, shepherds might expect to get hurt fighting a wolf, but they wouldn't expect to die to save a sheep. They would let the wolf have the sheep. Jesus talks about a different kind of shepherd. Let's read a verse about that. Ask a volunteer to read John 10:11.

- What kind of shepherd does Jesus say he is? *(The good shepherd.)*
- What does the good shepherd do that other shepherds don't? *(Gives his life for the sheep.)*
- If Jesus is the shepherd, what are we? *(Sheep.)*

In this chapter Jesus talks about the hired man who doesn't care about the sheep. When he sees a wolf coming, he runs away. He doesn't even try to keep the sheep safe. But the good shepherd is willing to give his own life to keep the sheep safe.

That's what Jesus did for us when he died for us. He made sure that we would be safe in God's care. He suffered so that we wouldn't have to. Let's pray and be thankful for what Jesus did.

Dear God, thank you for sending Jesus to be our good shepherd. Thank you that he loves us enough to die for us. Help us to be thankful for the good shepherd who loves us and keeps us safe. Amen.

Made Just Right

On Your Mark

Bible Truth: God made us in his image. We are valuable to him.

Bible Verse: LORD, you are our Father. We are the clay. You are the potter. Your hands made all of us. Isaiah 64:8

Godprint: Preciousness

Get Set

You'll need play dough or modeling clay and a surface to use it on, such as a vinyl tablecloth. Mark Isaiah 64:8 in your Bible. Optional: if you prefer a less messy option, put a small amount of clay in a zip-top bag for each child to manipulate inside the sealed bag.

GO!

Give every child a zip-top bag of clay or invite several children one at a time to manipulate a larger lump. **If I asked you to make something really valuable out of this clay, what would you make?** Pause for answers; if you have time and space, let some kids quickly mold something out of clay.

Now suppose I said I wanted you to make something out of the clay that would make people think of you. What would you make? Pause for answers or time to manipulate clay.

In Bible times, people called potters made things out of clay. They made pots and jars and lamps and bowls and all kinds of things that people used in their houses every day. Some of these things were very plain, some were fancy with designs and handles. The potter uses his hands to get just the right shape, molding the clay in just the right way.

- If you like what you make with clay and you want to keep it, what do you do? (*Let it dry.*)
- What do you think the potter would do if he didn't like the shape he was making? (*Smash down the clay and start over.*)

A good potter wants the pot to be perfect, even if it means starting over. The finished pot is no accident. It's on purpose, because the potter made it just right.

The Bible gives us a picture of God as a potter. Let's read a verse about that. Ask a volunteer to read Isaiah 64:8.

- What do you think it means to be the clay that God uses? *(God can make us into anything he wants us to be.)*
- Why is it important to remember that God is the potter who made us? *(God is our Father and loves us; he wants to make us into something good.)*

This verse calls God both our Father and the potter who made us. God made us just the way he wants us. The Bible says that God made us in his own image, to be like him. Nothing is more valuable than that! Think of something that is precious to you. God feels that way about you, but ten times more, a hundred times more, a thousand times more!

The next time you're using your hands with play dough or clay, or making a pot or sculpture of your own, I hope you'll remember that God made you with his own hands. And he made you just right!

Bow for prayer. **God, you are our Father and you are the potter who made us with your hands. Thank you for making us just right. We want you to make us into anything you want us to be. In Jesus' name, amen.**

Long Live the King

Bible Truth: God wants to be the true king of my life.

Bible Verse: How wonderful is the LORD Most High! He is the great King over the whole earth. Psalm 47:2

Godprint: Awe and wonder

Get Set

You'll need a crown made of aluminum foil and a wrapping paper tube wrapped in foil to use as a scepter. Mark Psalm 47:2 in your Bible. Optional: Decorate a big chair as a throne.

GO!

Da-da-da-daaa! The king has arrived. As children gather, put the crown on the head of one of the boys and hand him the scepter. Escort him to the throne if you have one. Bow deeply. **What is your desire, Your Highness? Your wish is our command.** Pause to let the "king" give a simple command that the rest of the children can obey, such as jump three times, or turn around once.

I hear the coronation trumpets sounding again. It's time to crown another king (or queen). Choose another child to receive the crown and scepter. Do this for as many children as time allows. Let each one give a simple command for the others to obey. Then set the crown and scepter aside.

It's fun to imagine being the king. We can pretend that we can have whatever we want and tell people what to do.

- Have you ever thought about what it might be like to have a king?
- Why do you think that some people would want to have a king, even *ask* to have a king?

The Bible is full of stories about kings. Can you name some? Pause for responses. Children may name Saul, David, Solomon, Ahab, Hezekiah and so on.

God's people in the Bible didn't always have a king. After God brought them out of slavery in Egypt and gave them their own land, they lived for a long time without a king. But many of them thought it was hard to live this way. If enemies tried to attack them, who

would lead them into battle? Wouldn't it be better if they got organized and had a leader they could depend on? They wanted to have a king like all the other countries. The people asked God for a king. Even though God didn't want them to have a human king, he gave them what they wanted. Saul became the first king.

When a new king was crowned, a trumpet sounded and everyone cried out, "Long live the king." The people sang special songs to celebrate the occasion. The king's job was to find out what God wanted for the people and lead the people in following God. Some of the kings did a good job at this, but a lot of others forgot about what they were supposed to do and just did whatever they wanted.

- Why do you suppose God didn't want the people to have a human king? *(Because he was their king.)*

Let's read a verse about the best king of all. Ask a volunteer to read Psalm 47:2.

- How much of the world is God the king over? *(All of it!)*
- Name some of the great things that God has done because he is king over the whole world.
- What do you think the world would be like if everyone believed that God was king?

We don't live in a country with a king. But we still have a king. God wants to be the true king in our lives. And he is a gr-r-r-eat king. He made the whole world and loves all the people in it.

Bow for prayer. **Lord, you are the great king over the whole earth. How amazing it is that the great king loves us and cares for us. Help us to love you and serve you. Thank you, Lord Most High. Amen.**

A House in Heaven

On Your Mark

Bible Truth: We can live with God forever in heaven.

Bible Verse: We know that the earthly tent we live in will be destroyed. But we have a building made by God. It is a house in heaven that lasts forever. Human hands did not build it. 2 Corinthians 5:1

Godprint: Hope

Get Set

You'll need a simple dome tent to set up, or some chairs and a blanket to make a tent. Mark 2 Corinthians 5:1 in your Bible.

GO!

Set the tent up before your presentation, or, if you have time, let kids help you set it up. Gather kids around the tent.

• What's the difference between a tent and a house?

One little boy answered that question by saying that a tent doesn't have a hallway and a house does! True enough. A tent doesn't have a lot of things that a house has. But you can do things with a tent that you can't do with a house, like pack it up and move it somewhere else. Take a moment to have kids help you move the tent to another location.

• What do you think tents were made of during Bible times?

Originally tents were made from animal skins. Later they were made from goats' hair. The hair from goats was woven into a cloth, and tentmakers could cut and sew the pieces of a tent together. Some famous people in the Bible were tentmakers. Their names were Aquila, Priscilla and Paul. Paul is the most famous, because he wrote many of the books of the New Testament. Paul was a great teacher and writer, and he helped to start many churches, but he earned his living by making tents.

Some people lived in tents all the time, especially in Old Testament days. But tents wear

out, don't they? They get holes in the side or rips in the seam. When a tent gets too old, we just can't use it any more. Remove a key pole to collapse your tent or pull the blanket off of the chairs.

Let's read a verse that Paul the tentmaker wrote about tents. Ask a volunteer to read 2 Corinthians 5:1.

- What do you think Paul means by "the earthly tent we live in"? (Our human bodies.)
- What will happen to our earthly tent? (It will be destroyed; the body wears out and we die.)
- Who made the house in heaven that lasts forever? (God.)

This verse tells us that we have a home in heaven with God. When these bodies that we're in today wear out, God will give us new bodies that will be just right for living with him in heaven forever. God gave us the Holy Spirit to live inside us while we live in our earthly bodies. God wants us to live with him forever, so he gives us a "house in heaven," a new body that will be perfect for living with God. What a great thing to look forward to!

Bow for prayer. Dear God, you made wonderful earthly bodies for us. But you have something even better for us in heaven. We look forward to being with you there and living with you forever. In Jesus' name, amen.

Holy, Holy, Holy

On Your Mark

Bible Truth: Because of Jesus' sacrifice, we can have a relationship with God.

Bible Verse: He isn't like the other high priests. They need to offer sacrifices day after day. First they bring tofferings for their own sins. Then they do it for the sins of the people. But Jesus gave one sacrifice for the sins of the people. He gave it once and for all time. He did it by offering himself.   Hebrews 7:27

Godprint: Faith

Get Set

Mark Hebrews 7:27 in your Bible.

GO!

As kids gather for the children's sermon, encourage them to remain standing while you arrange them. If you need more people, borrow some teenagers and adults from the congregation.

Arrange some of the kids in a half-circle in front of the congregation. They can face the congregation so they can listen as you talk. Arrange the rest of the kids in a second concentric half circle .

Congratulations! You've just made a living model of the main parts of the temple from the Bible.

Pause to see if anyone can identify the main parts, then continue your explanation. Move forward into the congregation and stand in the aisle.

The congregation represents the main part of the temple. At the time

of Jesus, this part of the temple had several sections—for Gentiles, for men, for women. But it was a part of the temple that lots of people could enter.

Move to the first half-circle of kids. **The next part of the temple was the Holy Place. Each morning and evening, a priest went into the Holy Place to offer sacrifices. The priest represented the people before God, but only the priests could go into the Holy Place. They made sacrifices every day to make the people acceptable to God.**

Move to the next half-circle. **Inside the Holy Place was the Most Holy Place. Only one person was allowed to go into this part of the temple: the high priest. Once a year, on the Day of Atonement, the high priest went into the Most Holy Place to ask God's forgiveness for the sins of the people.**

Have the kids gather and sit down. Let's read a verse in the New Testament that tells us about these sacrifices and something about Jesus. Ask a volunteer to read Hebrews 7:27.

- Why did the priests bring sacrifices day after day? (*Because the people sinned every day, even the priests.*)
- What sacrifice did Jesus give? (*Himself.*)

This verse tells us that Jesus was both the high priest and the sacrifice. And he was the last sacrifice anyone ever needed. Jesus never sinned, so he was the perfect sacrifice. Because Jesus died for us, we don't have to worry that God won't forgive our sins. We know that he will. We don't have to keep trying to be good enough for God to love us. Jesus did that for us. If we have faith in Jesus, we can have a relationship with God that lasts forever. That's pretty awesome, isn't it? It makes me feel like thanking God.

Bow for prayer. **God, you sent Jesus to be the best sacrifice of all, the one that would give us a relationship with you. Thank you for making a way that our sins can be forgiven once and for all. In Jesus' name, amen.**

Hear Ye, Hear Ye

On Your Mark

Bible Truth: God speaks to us; we can do his work.

Bible Verse: In the past, God spoke to our people through the prophets. He spoke at many times. He spoke in different ways. But in these last days, he has spoken to us through his Son. Hebrews 1:1–2a

Godprint: Commitment

Get Set

You'll need a megaphone or rolled up poster board. Mark Hebrews 1:1 in a Bible. Optional: Bible time costume, such as a robe and beard.

GO!

If you have a Bible time costume, put it on. As kids gather, put the megaphone to your mouth and speak through it. Use children's names with a brief message. **(Name), God loves you. (Name), God wants you to serve him. (Name), God will speak to you.**

I have an important message. Everyone needs to hear this message. I need your help spreading the message. So here's what I want you to do. I'll whisper the message to you, then you each go find one person to tell the message to. Then those people will tell the message to someone else. Then come back here, okay? Ready? Here's the message. Whisper. **God wants us to do his work.** Let the kids know they can get up to spread the message.

Gather the kids again. **In the Old Testament, a few people had a special job of telling the people what God wanted. They were called prophets. God spoke to a prophet and gave him a message. Then the prophet told the message to the king or to the people. Some prophets had groups of followers who helped spread the message, just like you did.**

The people didn't always listen to the message from God, because the message wasn't always something they wanted to hear. But God never stopped speaking to his people. Let's read a verse about that. Open your Bible and read Hebrews 1:1 and the first part of verse 2: "In the past, God spoke to our people through the prophets. He spoke at many times. He spoke in different ways. But in these last days, he has spoken to us through his Son."

- How did God speak in the past? *(Through prophets.)*
- Finish this sentence: In these last days, God has spoken to us through his _____ *(Son).*

In the Old Testament, the prophets did God's work by spreading his message. In the New Testament, Jesus did God's work by coming to earth, telling people about God's kingdom and dying so we could be part of God's kingdom. God's work isn't finished. He wants us to carry on and tell the Good News about Jesus to other people. He speaks to us through his Word and the Holy Spirit so we'll know what to do.

Let's pass the megaphone around. When it's your turn, call out something about Jesus that you want other people to know or say, something to praise God. Take the first turn yourself, then pass the megaphone to one of the kids. Let several kids have a turn, but don't make kids participate if they feel shy.

I think everyone heard you loud and clear! Maybe your job is speaking to people; maybe it's showing kindness or being a helper. Remember that God has a job for each of you. Let's listen for him in our hearts.

Bow for prayer. **Thank you for speaking to us through your Son and through your Word. We want to serve you and do your work. Help us to honor you with our lives and do the work that you give us to do. Amen.**

Goin' Fishin'

Bible Truth: God wants us to tell others about him.

Bible Verse: "Come. Follow me," Jesus said. "I will make you fishers of people." Matthew 4:19

Godprint: Evangelism

Get Set

You'll need a large blanket. Mark Matthew 4:19 in your Bible.

GO!

As kids gather, get out your blanket. **I'm going fishing today. Wanna come along? Oh, wait, I have an idea. You be the fish! Let me see your best fish face and your best fish wiggle.** Demonstrate by pushing your lips out in a fish face; put your palms together in front of you and move your arms through the air.

Keep going! I'm going to go fishing by throwing this net out over all the little fishies I see swimming around. If part of the blanket lands on you, then I've caught you! You can only "swim" by taking heel-to-toe baby steps.

Throw out the blanket and "catch" a few kids. Move your catch to one side. **How many did I catch?** Count the kids the blanket landed on. **Mmm. Maybe I need to try that again.** Toss out the blanket to catch some more fish.

Most of us think of fishing as something that we do for fun and relaxation. Maybe you've taken a fishing trip with your family. Maybe you've been fishing in a lake or a river, or maybe even the ocean.

In Bible times, a lot of people went fishing as a way to make a living. That was their job. During Jesus' time on earth, he traveled around the Sea of Galilee, which was a great place to go fishing. Many of Jesus' disciples were fishermen, and Jesus found them fishing on the Sea of Galilee. You probably use a pole when you go fishing. These fishermen used big nets. They threw them over the water. The nets would sink down around fish, then the fishermen would pull the net closed and haul it back to the boat to see what they caught.

Peter, Andrew, James and John were two sets of brothers. They were ordinary fishermen. Then Jesus called them to follow him. Let's read about that. Ask a volunteer to read Matthew 4:19.

- What did Jesus say to the fishermen?
- What does it mean to fish for people?

Peter, Andrew, James and John—and all the other disciples—were ordinary people doing ordinary, everyday things. Jesus gave them a job to do. The Bible says they left their fishing nets and followed Jesus. And when we follow Jesus, we have the same job to do. God wants us to tell others about him so they can follow Jesus, too.

- If you were going to tell someone about Jesus, what would you say?

The next time you go fishing, or the next time you see a fish, remember that Jesus wants you to fish for people!

Bow for prayer. **Lord, you called the fishermen from the Sea of Galilee, and you call each of us. There are so many people who need to be "caught" for you. Help us to fish for people and let everyone we meet know about God's love. In Jesus' name, amen.**

Seeds of Generosity

On Your Mark

Bible Truth: God wants us to be generous with other people.

Bible Verse: Here is something to remember. The one who plants only a little will gather only a little. And the one who plants a lot will gather a lot. 2 Corinthians 9:6

Godprint: Generosity

Get Set

You'll need a small packet of seeds and a small bowl. Mark 2 Corinthians 9:6 in your Bible. Optional: pot with potting soil, gardening gloves, hat and tools.

GO!

If you have a big sun hat and gardening gloves, wear them. As kids gather, shake the packet of seeds.

Look what I've got here. A great big flowerbed full of gorgeous spring flowers. Yes sirree, that's what I've got. Pause to look at the kids. **You don't look convinced.** Some kids may point out that you just have seeds, not flowers.

Let's find out exactly what we've got here. Open the packet of seeds and pour the seeds into your hand. **I need someone to help me count these seeds.** Depending on the size of your group, you may choose one helper or several. Have the kids count the seeds as they transfer them from your hand to the bowl.

- How many of these seeds do you think I should plant? One? Two?
- Why should I plant all of the seeds?

People who live in towns or cities might have flower beds or vegetable gardens. It doesn't take too many seeds to grow those. People who live on farms and grow fields of crops need a lot more seeds. In Bible times, many people were farmers. Getting the land ready to plant was a big job. When harvest time came, the farmers would be busy again.

What do you suppose would happen if they scattered a few seeds like these over the whole farm field? They'd only get a few plants. If they wanted a big harvest, they had to

plant a lot of seeds. Let's read a verse in the Bible about planting and harvesting. Ask a volunteer to read 2 Corinthians 9:6.

- What happens to the farmer who plants only a little?
- What happens to the farmer who plants a lot?

The Apostle Paul wrote this verse. He was writing to some people who weren't sure they wanted to share what they had with others. He wanted them to know that if they were generous, it would be like planting a lot of seeds; they would get a big harvest. But if they were selfish, it would be like planting only a few seeds in a big field; they would get a small harvest.

- What happens when you share what you have generously?

God wants us to give generously—plant lots of seeds! And he wants us to give cheerfully. God gives generously to us. Everything we have comes from God. He makes sure we have what we need so we can be generous with other people.

Optional: If you have a pot and potting soil, have a helper or two plant a few seeds. Tell the kids you'll keep the pot in a place where they can watch the plant grow as a reminder that God wants us to plant generously.

Bow for prayer. **God, we thank you for everything that you give to us. Make us grateful and glad to share. Help us see where we can plant seeds of generosity with other people because you are generous with us. In your name we pray, amen.**

Good Guy, Bad Job

On Your Mark

Bible Truth: God helps us turn away from selfishness and be more like him.

Bible Verse: The Son of Man came to look for the lost and save them. Luke 19:10

Godprint: Repentance

Get Set

You'll need a big shopping bag or duffel bag, an assortment of small toys and a supply of wrapped candy or other treat. Ask someone to be your assistant. Put the bag of treats in the shopping bag. Mark Luke 19:10 in your Bible.

GO!

As kids assemble, have your assistant pass out small toys to the first to arrive. Not every child needs one—though they may all want one. When all the kids are gathered, look around at the kids with toys.

Hey, where did you get that toy? I don't have a toy like that. I want that toy! Snatch the toys from the kids and stuff them into your bag. **Those are my toys and I don't want you to have them! I'm not going to share!** Hang on to your bag tightly. You may get some blank looks, but you'll also get some objections.

- Why do you think I took those toys away from you? (*Selfishness.*)
- How did you feel when I took the toys?
- Can you think of a Bible story about selfishness? (*Kids may have several ideas; focus on Zacchaeus from Luke 19.*)

Zacchaeus was a tax collector at the time when Jesus lived on earth. Not many people liked tax collectors, but it was a good job for a selfish person. Tax collectors worked for the Roman government. Their job was to collect the taxes that everyone owed to the government and turn it in. That was bad enough, because people didn't like the Roman government. But if you were a tax collector, you got to take more money from people than they really owed and keep the extra for yourself. The Romans didn't care how much extra you took. So a lot of tax collectors took way too much! They didn't just do a job that nobody liked, they did it in a selfish way.

• Who remembers what happened when Zacchaeus met Jesus? *(Zacchaeus was in a tree because he was short, and Jesus called him down. Jesus went to Zacchaeus's house and showed that he cared about Zacchaeus; Zacchaeus promised to give back four times as much as he took from people.)*

Zacchaeus decided to give back what he had taken! In fact, he decided to give back *more* than he had taken. Mmm. Maybe I should do something like what Zacchaeus did. I took some things selfishly. Maybe I need to give back generously. Reach into your bag and pull out the treats. Let every child have one.

Let's read the last verse in the story of Zacchaeus. Ask a volunteer to read Luke 19:10 as kids enjoy their treats.

• Jesus is the Son of Man. What does this verse say Jesus came for? *(To look for the lost and save them.)*
• What made the change in Zacchaeus? *(He wanted to be like Jesus; he was sorry for what he'd done.)*

When Zacchaeus met Jesus, he realized his selfish ways were wrong, and he wanted to change them. He wanted to do things God's way instead. Zacchaeus turned away from himself and turned toward God. That's what we call "repenting."

God wants us to do the same thing—turn away from our sins, and turn toward him. We're all lost without Jesus. He's the one who shows us the way to God. Jesus helped Zacchaeus change from the inside out. He can do the same thing for us—we just have to ask.

Bow for prayer. **Lord, you are the one we want to be like. Help us to turn away from thinking only about ourselves. Help us to turn toward you so that we can be more and more like you. In Jesus' name we pray, amen.**

Hammer, Hammer, Saw, Saw

On Your Mark

Bible Truth: God has a plan for us and helps us "build" our lives.

Bible Verse: If the LORD doesn't build a house, the work of its builders is useless. Psalm 127:1

Godprint: Purposefulness

Get Set

You'll need blocks or something else that the kids can build with quickly. Mark Psalm 127:1 in your Bible.

GO!

When the children have gathered, dump the blocks in front of them. If you have a large group, you might want to select just a few kids for the building project. If your group is small, everyone can participate.

When I say, "Go," I want you to build something together really fast. When I say, "Stop," you have to stop, even if you're not finished. Are you ready? Go!

Allow a minute or so for kids to build something. Some of them may work extra fast because they don't know how much time they really have. Others will have a hard time trying to keep up. That's okay. Call **Stop.**

Let's see. How did you do? Exaggerate your inspection of the final product and make some wild guesses about what it might be. Chances are it won't look like much of anything because of the lack of opportunity to plan or work systematically in a short period of time.

- How did you feel about having to build something together without planning what it would be?
- Are you happy with what you ended up with?

I think we could have used a carpenter to help us out, don't you? Someone who knows how to build and perhaps had a few tools might have been a great help.

Can you think of any carpenters in the Bible? *(Joseph was a carpenter; Jesus likely learned the carpentry trade from him.)*

In Bible times, many things were made of wood. Wagons and wheels and carts for working were made of wood. Some tools were made from wood or had wood handles. And of course furniture was made from wood. People needed the things that a carpenter could make. Joseph was a carpenter, so as Jesus grew up he learned to be a carpenter, too.

- How can a carpenter make sure that what he builds will last? *(Good planning, good materials, right tools, skill and experience.)*

Let's read a verse about good building. Find Psalm 127:1 in your Bible and read the first part: "If the LORD doesn't build a house, the work of its builders is useless."

Look for the youngest or smallest child in your group. **I would like (child's name) to come up here and do something for me.** When the child comes close, whisper in his or her ear to knock down what the others have built.

Whoa! That sure didn't last, did it? It's like everything we did was a wasted effort. Remember the verse we read? "If the LORD doesn't build a house, the work of its builders is useless." Is this verse talking about an actual building? No. This verse reminds us that the best plans are the Lord's plans. Sometimes we rush around doing things in a hurry or our own way, and we don't take time to do them right or to find out what God's plans are. When we do that, things don't work out. It's just like having our building kicked down.

God is the best carpenter of all. He has a plan for our lives and will help us build our lives according to that plan. Our part is to slow down and find out what God's plan is before we start building.

Bow for prayer. **Lord, thank you for having a plan for our lives. Help us to slow down and find out what the plan is. Build our lives into a house that will honor you. Amen.**

Down and Up

On Your Mark

Bible Truth: God wants us to think about others, not just ourselves.

Bible Verse: Everyone who lifts himself up will be brought down. And anyone who is brought down will be lifted up. Luke 18:14.

Godprint: Humility

Get Set

You'll need a bag of cotton balls. Mark Luke 18:14 in your Bible.

GO!

As children gather, give each one a cotton ball. **I want you to put this cotton ball on the end of your nose and make it stay there. How do you think you can do that?** Pause to let kids try. They'll end up tilting their heads back with their noses in the air to try to keep the cotton balls balanced on their faces.

Look at all of you with your noses in the air! You can hold your cotton balls in your laps now.

That reminds me of a story that Jesus told. Two men went to the temple to pray. One of them was a Pharisee, a very religious person, and the other was a tax collector. Remember, most people thought tax collectors were awful sinners. The Pharisee prayed out loud something like this: "God, thank you that I'm not like all those other people, especially this tax collector. I'm very religious and do all the things the law says to do." Then the tax collector prayed. He said, "God, have mercy on me, a sinner."

• Which man do you think pleased God more? *(The tax collector.)* Why?

The Pharisees were a group of people who wanted to be sure they did everything right all the time so they would never break God's law. To make sure that they didn't break God's law, they made up lots and lots of extra rules about what people should and shouldn't do. The Pharisees thought they were better than anyone else because they followed all these extra little rules. They thought that people who didn't follow their rules could never please God.

When Jesus lived on earth, he wanted the people to know that God gave the law because he loved his people. The law was a way for people to know God. It wasn't supposed to be a burden that made it hard to please God.

Put your cotton balls back on your noses.

- What happens when you try to look at the people around you? *(It's hard! The cotton ball will fall off.)*
- How is having a cotton ball on your nose like being a Pharisee?

The Pharisee who prayed in the temple had his nose up in the air. He was so proud of himself, and he went to the temple to pray out loud so that everyone there could see how proud he was. He was so busy being religious that he didn't think about other people.

- Why did the tax collector go to the temple to pray? *(Because he knew he was a sinner.)*

Let's find out what Jesus had to say after he finished telling this story. Open your Bible to Luke 18 and read the end of verse 14: "Everyone who lifts himself up will be brought down. And anyone who is brought down will be lifted up."

- What does it mean to "lift yourself up"? *(Be too proud, think you are better than other people.)*
- What does it mean to be "brought down"? *(To be humbled; to find out you're not as great as you thought you were.)*
- How can being humble help you care about other people?

Jesus wants us to have soft, humble hearts, not proud hearts like the Pharisee. Keep your cotton ball as a reminder to be soft and humble toward God and toward others.

Bow for prayer. **Lord, have mercy on us, because we are sinners. Help us not to be so proud that we can't be kind to other people. Help us to remember that we always need you. Amen.**

Don't Forget

On Your Mark

Bible Truth: Knowing God's Word helps us be loyal to him.

Bible Verse: My son, obey my words. Store up my commands inside you. Obey my commands and you will live. Guard my teachings as you would your own eyes. Tie them on your fingers. Write them on the tablet of your heart. Proverbs 7:1–3

Godprint: Loyalty

Get Set

You'll need a supply of string and scissors, a piece of paper and a pencil. Make copies of the heart tablets on page 110. Mark Proverbs 7:1–3 in your Bible.

GO!

If you have a large group, plan to have a couple of assistants (older kids or adults) to help you tie strings on kids' fingers at the end. You might want to cut some lengths of string ahead of time.

As kids gather, get out the string and start trying to tie a piece of string around each of your fingers. You'll probably need some extra hands, so ask a couple of the kids to help you tie knots and cut string. Mutter as you work. **I'm so afraid I'll forget. It seems like I can't remember what I was thinking just a minute ago. But I've heard this will really help my memory.** Keep going until you have a piece of string hanging from each finger of one hand.

There. Now I'll remember. Flap your strings. **Now, what was it I was supposed to remember? Oh, yes, now I remember. Maybe I'd better write that down before I forget.** Take out your paper and pencil and scribble something down. Write down something like a phone number you need to call or a few items you need to buy at the grocery store, and let kids know what you're writing.

• What do you do when you need to remember something really important?

Do you ever have to write your spelling words 10 times? Or copy down a paragraph from the blackboard at school? Writing something down can be a great way to help you remember. What about tying a string on your finger? How can that help? (*Every time you see the string, you remember why you put it there.*)

In Bible times, not everyone knew how to read and write. Certain men were trained as scribes. Their job was to write down important things, like contracts or letters. They also made copies of God's Word. Can you imagine copying a whole book with your pencil and paper? It's not easy work. The scribes copied carefully to be sure they didn't make mistakes. They did this so more people could know what God's Word said and live the way God wanted them to live.

Let's read a verse about remembering God's Word. Ask a volunteer to read Proverbs 7:1–3.

- What do these verses say we should do with God's Word? *(Store it inside us. Obey it. Guard it. Tie God's teachings on fingers and write down God's commands.)*
- Why does God want us to do these things? *(So we can know how he wants us to live. So that we won't forget what his Word says.)*

Wow. I guess these strings can remind me of something more important than my grocery list. I'd like you to tie a string to your finger to help you remember to remember God's Word. If your group is large, invite your assistants to help.

The Bible verse also said to write God's commands on the tablets of our hearts. I'm going to give you a picture of a "heart tablet" so you can copy down some of your favorite Bible verses and keep them in a place where you can see them whenever you want. Pass out copies of page 110.

- What do you think you'll put on your heart tablet?

Bow for prayer. **Dear God, thank you for giving us your Word. Help us to remember your teachings even without tying them on our fingers. We want to obey you and live the way you want us to live. In your name we pray, amen.**

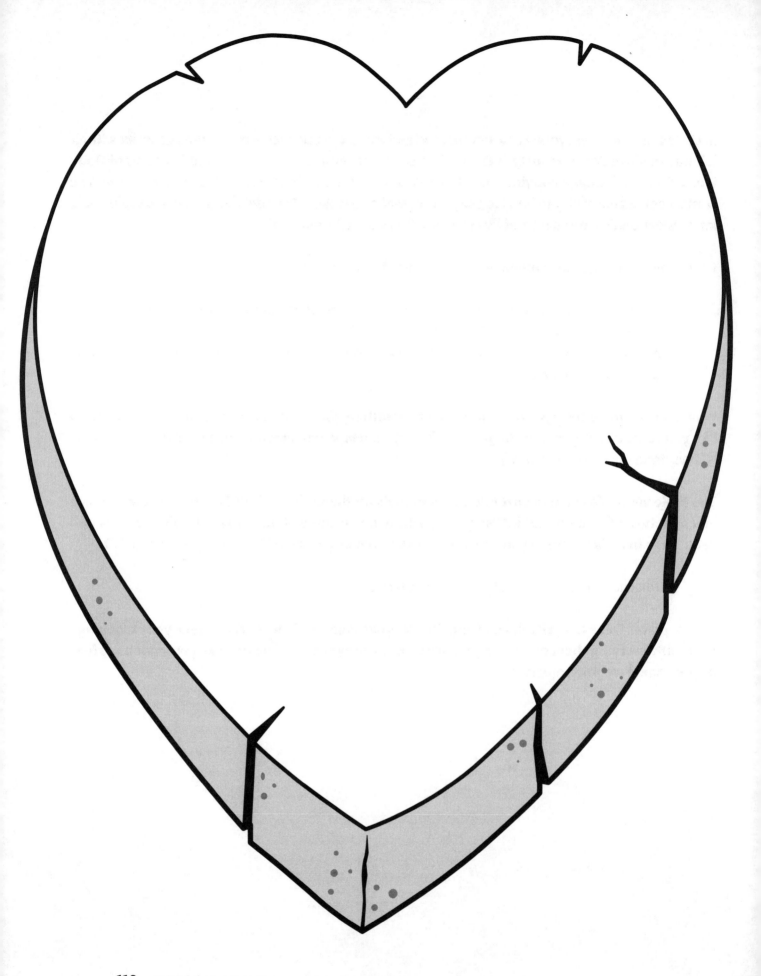

Index of Godprints and Topics

Index of Scripture References